A BRIEF LIFE OF
THE QUEEN

A BRIEF LIFE OF
THE QUEEN

by

Robert Lacey

Duckworth Overlook

First published in the UK in 2012 by Duckworth Overlook

LONDON

90-93 Cowcross Street

London EC1M 6BF

Tel: 020 7490 7300

Fax: 020 7490 0080

info@duckworth-publishers.co.uk

www.ducknet.co.uk

A catalogue record for this book is
available from the British Library

ISBN 978 07156 4292 4

Page design by Crispin Goodall Design
Printed in the UK by the
MPG Books Group, Bodmin, Cornwall

Contents

'The most profound satisfaction that royalty provides is that it gives us a paradise to inhabit.'
Virginia Woolf, 1939

'As far as I can see, some people have to be fed royalty like sea-lions fish.'
Cecilia Bowes-Lyon, Countess of Strathmore,
Grandmother of Queen Elizabeth II

Acknowledgements

I have been writing about the Queen now for nearly forty years, and this little book is intended to distill and reshape what I've learned into one pleasant afternoon's reading – a summary of its predecessors *Majesty* (1977) and *Monarch* (2002, *Royal* in the UK), with further research and thoughts on Elizabeth II as her Diamond Jubilee approaches.

The two previous volumes contain lengthy notes, bibliographies and acknowledgements setting out my methods and sources, together with my gratitude to the hundreds of friends and contacts developed over my years studying the monarchy.

For their additional help with this *Brief Life* I should also like to thank my family, Walter Arnstein, Jennifer Barth, Mink Choi, Anne De Courcy, Carmen Dell'Orefice, Susie Dowdall, Ben Dyal, Eileen Ford, Grainne Fox, Suzanne Hodgart, Jon Jackson, Tim Jennings, Richard Kay, Lonson MacCargar, Peter Mayer, Jane Mays, Donal McMahon, Diana Melly, Peter Morgan, Andrew Morton, Matt Nieman Sims, Sandra Parsons, Jonathan Pegg, Simon Perry, Bill Phillips, David Pogson, Jane Rayne, Nigel Rees, Edda Tasiemka, Yvonne Ward, Jacqueline Williams and Kenneth Rose CBE, the royal biographer whose insight and wit has set the standard for the rest of us – and to whom this book is dedicated.

Robert Lacey
November, 2011

To Kenneth Rose

List of Illustrations

Working Together

1

Princess of Hearts
1926–1947

When the future Queen of the United Kingdom, Australia, Canada, New Zealand and a dozen other Commonwealth countries* was first learning to talk, she had difficulty pronouncing all the syllables in Elizabeth. 'Lilibet' was the best she could manage, so that became the name by which her family knew her throughout her childhood and, in the case of her husband Prince Philip, to this day – though when he's feeling particularly affectionate, he also calls her 'Cabbage'.

Little Lilibet loved to ride her tricycle. To judge from her tailored coat and sensible shoes, she might have been any well-born three-year-old pedalling the gravelled gardens of Mayfair at the end of the 1920s. Except that she called her grandfather 'Grandpa England' – and he lived across the park in Buckingham Palace.

Elizabeth of York was not born to be Queen. She came into the world on 23rd April 1926, the equivalent of the modern Princess Beatrice: first-born daughter of the Duke of York, destined to flutter on the royal fringe. York is the dukedom traditionally given to the monarch's second son – Prince Andrew today and Elizabeth's father, Prince Albert,

---

* The twelve other realms are Jamaica, Barbados, the Bahamas, Grenada, Papua New Guinea, the Solomon Islands, Tuvalu, St. Lucia, St. Vincent and the Grenadines, Belize, Antigua and Barbuda, and St. Kitts and Nevis. Then there are 34 other nations – India, Nigeria, Pakistan and South Africa among them – who recognise Elizabeth II as Head of the Commonwealth.

BIKER.
Princess Elizabeth of York rides her tricycle in Hamilton Gardens, Mayfair. 1931

in the 1920s. So while Lilibet was brought up with almost religious respect for the crown, there seemed no chance of her inheriting it. Her young head was never turned by the personal prospect of grandeur – which is why she would prove so very good at her job. Elizabeth II's lack of ego was to prove the paradoxical secret of her greatness.

She grew up in no. 145 Piccadilly, a large, semi-detached London town house that was destroyed by German bombs in World War II and is now the site of the London Intercontinental Hotel beside the Hard Rock Café. Her nursery was at the top of the house, stocked with dark, polished, grown-up furniture, complete with a clock and a glass-fronted display case. The night nursery in which she slept had no plumbing – there was a large jug and a basin holding water to wash her hands. On the landing outside the Princess took to collecting the toy horses on wheels she liked to ride around the house. Every evening she would change their saddles and harnesses before she went to bed.

We know these details thanks to Lady Cynthia Asquith and Anne Ring, confidantes of Elizabeth's PR-conscious mother, the Duchess of York, who handed over family photographs and encouraged the ladies to write syrupy articles and books to feed the public appetite for 'intimate and authentic' details of royal life. With royal sanction, the writers took their readers on a tour of the plum-carpeted premises of no. 145 so they could see the rocking horses on the landing and could almost touch the little scarlet dustpan and brush with which the Princess was taught to keep her room tidy. They were even invited inside the bathroom to imagine the naked splashings of a 'damp, pink chcrub who seemed to be finding this bathing business the perfect end to what had been a perfect day.'

With a voyeuristic emphasis on domestic furnishings, Lady Cynthia and Ms Ring developed a style of public intimacy which suggested that the Duchess of York had thoroughly absorbed her mother's opinions on royalty, fish and sea-lions. When it was let slip that the Princess's nursery clothes and trimmings were in yellow, other colours fell out of favour overnight. Until then customers at Selfridges of Oxford Street had had to order specially if they wanted something other than pink or blue for their children. 'Now almost every mother wants to buy a little yellow frock or a primrose bonnet like Princess Elizabeth's,' reported America's *TIME* Magazine, which chose to put the Princess on its cover in April 1929 for setting a major fashion trend when she was only three.

The Royal Family doted on the little Princess as much as did the general public. When King George V fell ill with bronchial pneumonia early in 1929, his doctors prescribed recuperation in the bracing sea air of Bognor on the Sussex coast, and his granddaughter was sent down to aid his recovery.

'G. delighted to see her,' wrote Queen Mary in her diary at the end of March 1929. 'I played ... in the garden making

COVER GIRL.
Princess Elizabeth aged 3, featured in TIME *Magazine for 29ᵗʰ April 1929*

sandpies! The Archbishop of Canterbury came to see us and was so kind and sympathetic.'

When the King got back to London he maintained that regular contact with his granddaughter was essential to his health and worked out that, before the leaves were on the trees in Green Park, he could actually see the front windows of no. 145 Piccadilly from Buckingham Palace. So every winter morning, soon after breakfast, the young Princess would draw her curtains and wave across the park, while her grandfather looked out for her and waved back.

On 21st August 1930 Elizabeth was joined by a younger sister, Princess Margaret Rose, who, at the age of three weeks, was described by her delighted mother as already possessing a will of iron to complement her large blue eyes – 'all the equipment that a lady needs!' The wayward consequences of Margaret's iron will were to generate no little trouble and controversy in Elizabeth's adult life, but in 1930 the immediate upshot of her arrival was rearrangement in the nursery. Elizabeth's existing nanny 'Alla', Clara Knight, an elderly, square-jawed country woman who had served as nanny to the Duchess herself thirty years earlier, now took charge of the new arrival, leaving the four-year-old Princess to the care of her young Scottish assistant, Margaret 'Bobo' MacDonald, the twenty-six-year-old daughter of an Inverness railway worker.

For the next six decades Bobo MacDonald was to become closer to Elizabeth than anyone else from outside her family – her most intimate companion and confidante. The plain-spoken young Scotswoman slept in the Princess's bedroom for most of her childhood then continued, as her dresser, to lay out her clothes every morning and evening in adult life – a legendary and rather feared power in the palace, credited with everything from her mistress's lamentably un-matching handbags to the Queen's notorious frugality. The young woman who had grown up in a company cottage beside a railway line trained Elizabeth to save the wrapping paper from her presents after Christmas and birthdays, to be neatly smoothed and stored away in a special box, with the gift ribbon rolled up for future use.

The parsimony was in keeping with the times. In September 1931 the worldwide slump accompanying the

Wall Street Crash forced Britain off the gold standard – the pound was devalued by 30 per cent – and confronted the Royal Family with the challenge it was to face at regular intervals throughout the life of Elizabeth: how to display sacrifice (the regularly deployed phrase was 'tighten the belt') and appear to share in the national suffering without raising questions about the extraordinary comfort and privilege they continued to enjoy. For the Yorks this took the form of the Duke giving up his beloved fox hunting and selling his horses – 'the parting with them,' he wrote, 'will be terrible' – while his daughters set to work with their dustpans and brushes.

In the grounds of Royal Lodge, the spacious Grace and Favour mansion where the Yorks spent their weekends in Windsor Great Park, stood *Y Bwythyn Bach*, 'The Little House', a present from the people of Wales. Built of Welsh materials by Welsh craftspeople, some of the most crucially hit labourers in the depression, *Y Bwythyn Bach* was a propaganda, make-work project first exhibited at the Ideal Home Exhibition in Olympia, then transferred to Windsor where it was photographed for morale-raising magazine features in which the little Princesses acted out the role of apprentice housewives. Everything was carefully constructed to two-thirds scale, from the wireless set on the miniature dresser to the packet of Epsom Salts in the bathroom – royals needed to be regular like everybody else.

Model house, model family – the messages were manifold: the Royal Family sympathised, honest Welsh labour could overcome, domestic virtues were worth celebrating and would triumph. The Little House was a parable not just for Wales but for the economic distress of the whole country. As fairy tales tame frightening realities, so the Goldilocks scale of the cottage helped make a desperate situation seem more manageable. The reigns of Queen Victoria and King Edward VII had emphasised the splendour of royal folk. Now Elizabeth and Margaret tidied for Britain as

LITTLE PRINCESSES.
Margaret and Elizabeth in front of Y Bwthyn Bach, *'The Little House', a gift from the people of Wales. 1933*

their grandfather George V sought to blend grandeur with ordinariness. In the summer of 1935 the old King celebrated his quarter of a century on the throne with a Silver Jubilee service. Troops from every corner of the Empire marched through flag-bedecked streets and cheering crowds, where the author George Orwell noted placards that proclaimed 'Long Live the King! Down with the Landlord!'

'It was even possible to see,' wrote the radical old Etonian, who had chosen to live as a beggar in London's East End for a time while researching his classic work of reportage, *Down and Out in Paris and London,* 'the survival, or recrudescence, of an idea almost as old as history, the idea of the King and the common people being in a sort of alliance against the upper classes.'

Such improbable identification – based in part at least, according to Orwell, on shared envy and fear – depended on a willing suspension of disbelief, and that willingness evaporated with extraordinary rapidity when George V died in January 1936, to be succeeded by his eldest son David, who took the title of Edward VIII. The new King had been a long-serving and brilliantly popular Prince of Wales, but he now set about flamboyantly sabotaging the conventions that had made him what he was:

> *Old men who never cheated, never doubted,*
> *Communicated monthly, sit and stare*
> *At a red suburb ruled by Mrs Simpson,*
> *Where a young man lands hatless from the air.*
>
> John Betjeman, *On the Death of King George V*

When MPs went down to their constituencies early in December 1936 to discuss the astonishing news that the new King's choice of wife and queen was a twice-married American socialite, Mrs Wallis Simpson, the grassroots reaction was unanimous.

'Our people won't 'ave it,' declared Ernest Bevin, the leader of the Transport and General Workers' Union.

'Whatever other position in society she may adorn,' declared the *Birmingham Post* in a scathing editorial on 7th December 1936, Mrs Simpson 'is not the person to become Queen of England.'

be placed on an easel in the Buckingham Palace schoolroom and through the spring of 1937 she gave lectures to her granddaughters to explain the role and symbolism of every participant.

In the Royal Archives, tied in pink ribbon, is Princess Elizabeth's own account of her parents' Coronation, written in her neat, rounded hand: 'To Mummy and Papa, In Memory of Their Coronation, From Lilibet. By Herself.' On 12th May 1937 – the date originally set for the crowning of Edward VIII – the eleven-year-old Princess was woken at 5.00 am by the band of the Royal Marines striking up outside the bedroom that she shared with her maid, the Inverness railwayman's daughter.

'I leapt out of bed,' she wrote, 'and so did Bobo. We put on dressing-gowns and shoes and Bobo made me put on an eiderdown as it was so cold, and we crouched in the window looking on to a cold, misty morning.'

After breakfast 'we went along to Mummy's bedroom and we found her putting on her dress. Papa was dressed in a white shirt, breeches and stockings, and over this he wore a crimson satin coat. Then a page came and said it was time to go down, so we kissed Mummy and wished her good luck and went down.'

Arriving at Westminster Abbey after a carriage ride that was 'very jolty,' the little girls processed down the aisle in their coronets and long silk dresses to enter the royal box with Queen Mary.

'I thought that it was all very, very wonderful and I expect the Abbey did, too. The arches and beams at the top were covered with a sort of haze of wonder as Papa was crowned, at least I thought so ... When Mummy was crowned and all the peeresses put on their coronets it looked wonderful to see arms and coronets hovering in the air and then arms disappear as if by magic.'

After nearly two and a half hours it was not, perhaps, surprising that the eleven-year-old found the proceedings 'rather boring ... it was all prayers. Grannie and I were looking to see how many more pages to the end, and we turned one more and then I pointed to the word at the bottom of the page and it said "Finis". We both smiled at each other.'

Around the country 132 volunteers were similarly noting their doings and emotions on this extraordinary day. January 1937 had seen the creation of an ambitious grassroots social research organisation to chart national feeling, 'Mass Observation' – 'an anthropology of our own people ... a sounding of the English collective unconscious' – and Coronation Day seemed the ideal opportunity to attempt the first ever popular investigation of Britain's feelings about royal ritual and the Royal Family. Most of the volunteer observers were left-wing and avowedly republican, but that did not stop them being strangely moved.

'I felt a definite pride and thrill in belonging to the Empire,' recorded one thirty-nine-year-old typist, 'which, in ordinary life, with my political bias, is just the opposite of my true feelings.'

'At each village there were celebrations in the open air, dancing, sports, brass bands ...' reported a bicycling republican from South Norwood who had pedalled down to the Kent-Sussex border, 'spontaneous merry-making that we saw, probably little changed from what it was centuries ago.'

A staunch Blackpool republican even encountered his own version of Princess Elizabeth's mystical haze of wonder. 'A strange thrill – apparently quite disconnected from everything – passed through me,' he recorded. 'I was annoyed, and a little afterwards wondered why.'

Educating Elizabeth was a process on which her parents pursued very different courses. George VI favoured the strictly vocational view promoted by his mother – even when Queen Mary gave her granddaughter a set of building bricks, each wooden brick in the box was sourced from a different country of the British Empire. But the Princesses' own mother, Queen Elizabeth, took a less rigorous approach. Her educational priorities, according to her official biographer, were 'plenty of fresh air, exercise, fun – and light reading.' So the Royal Librarian, Owen Morshead, was appalled to discover one July that the eighteen books that the Queen had ordered for her elder daughter's summer reading list were all novels – and every one of them by P.G. Wodehouse.

Trying to adjudicate, while also trying to advance her own quite ambitious educational agenda, was the Princesses' governess, Marion Crawford, another Scottish retainer who was inevitably given her own nickname – 'Crawfie'. A serious-minded, academically trained teacher, Crawfie soon found herself politely at odds with her mistress. 'Things are not made easy for me,' she complained to Lady Cynthia Colville. 'I have been more or less commanded to keep the afternoons as free of 'serious' work as possible.'

Crawfie took a trick from Queen Mary's book. She tried giving her charges an educational card game of Happy Families Around the World to take downstairs when they went to see their parents after tea. 'But I am afraid if I am not there to play too,' she reported, 'Racing Demon [a raucous, fast-paced, double-patience contest] wins the day!'

Owen Morshead weighed in on Crawfie's side, informing Queen Mary that the governess 'was apt to feel discouraged about her work from time to time ... [a] delicate point in which I know Your Majesty's feelings are deeply engaged.' With the old Queen's approval – and with Crawfie's willing collaboration – the librarian started giving the Princesses tours of Windsor Castle that doubled as constitutional history lessons.

But even this proved problematic.

'Between ourselves,' wrote Queen Mary to Morshead, 'I asked nice Miss Crawford about your talks to the Princesses which she is so keen about, [but] she says it is so awkward to fix definite hours or days for these, as her dear Majesty [Queen Elizabeth] constantly wants the children at odd moments.' This was 'a fatal proceeding when one has lessons to do,' opined the old Queen, 'and one which the late King and I never indulged in where lessons were concerned!'

How 'fatal' was a matter of opinion, however. Among the private papers and jottings of Queen Elizabeth, later the Queen Mother, was a poignant personal note of child-raising principles that she wrote out for her husband sometime in the 1930s 'in case of anything happening to me':

1. Be very careful not to ridicule your children or laugh at them ...

2. Always try and talk very quietly to children. Never shout or frighten them, as otherwise you lose their delightful trust in you.

3. Remember how your father, by shouting at you, and making you feel uncomfortable, lost all your real affection. None of his sons are his friends, because he is not understanding and helpful to them.

'None of his sons are his friends' is a chilling confession to emerge from the heart of any family – let alone from a family that justified its existence as an official exemplar of affectionate family life. In 2009 Queen Elizabeth II reviewed the hitherto private thoughts and writings of her mother in William Shawcross's official biography, and allowed these revealing and damning words to stand – suggesting that she endorsed the human values being championed when her mother decreed that time with parents was more important than time in the schoolroom. In the grand scheme of things, perhaps she also felt that reading the novels of P.G. Wodehouse every summer had not been such a disaster.

COMING OF AGE.
Princess Elizabeth and her mother Queen Elizabeth at Royal Lodge, Windsor,
April 1940

It was sometime in her thirteenth year that Princess Elizabeth went from girl to woman. 'Princess Elizabeth is growing up' ran the caption to an April 1939 photograph that made clear she had inherited her mother's generous bosom. Five months later Britain was at war and the demands on the teenager intensified. In 1938 Buckingham Palace had snootily rejected an American suggestion that the British Princesses might strengthen transatlantic friendship by making a brief radio contribution to National Children's Week in the US.

'There is, of course, no question of the Princesses broadcasting,' wrote their father's Private Secretary, Alan 'Tommy' Lascelles (pronounced to rhyme with 'tassels'), 'nor is it likely to be considered for many years to come.'

The idea seemed less preposterous with the Battle of Britain being fought overhead.

'Thousands of you have had to leave your homes and be separated from your fathers and mothers,' declared Princess Elizabeth in October 1940 in a broadcast that was syndicated around the world. 'My sister Margaret Rose and I feel so much for you, as we know from experience what it means to be away from those we love most of all ... My sister is by my side, and we are both going to say good night to you. Come on, Margaret!'

The ten-year-old leaned forward to do her bit.

'Good night!' piped her clearly younger voice. 'Good night and good luck to you all!'

Listening to the broadcast, Winston Churchill's Private Secretary, John 'Jock' Colville, expressed himself 'embarrassed by the sloppy sentiment,' but radio switchboards across America were jammed with requests for repeats, and the BBC turned the recording into a best-selling phonograph record. Schmaltz got results – and royal schmaltz did even better. In a time of danger, people yearned for reassurance from on high.

The reporters of Mass Observation – co-opted with the outbreak of war to monitor the national mood for the Ministry of Information – were able to prove it with figures. Surveying the output of the five newsreel companies serving British cinemas in 1939, they discovered that, following the opening of hostilities, the proportion of stories featuring members of the Royal Family had risen dramatically from 23 per cent to as high as 80 per cent in some bulletins.

Mistrustful of George Gallup's Q&A polling which had just arrived from America – they believed that people were more honest in the dark – the Mass Observers took their clipboards and stopwatches into cinemas to chart the applause. One speech by the stuttering George VI, complete with hesitant pauses, earned no less than seventeen seconds of clapping shortly after German bombers attacked

Buckingham Palace in September 1940, while even the exiled Duke of Windsor, installed as Governor of the Bahamas in military uniform the previous month, earned seven seconds of applause in one West End cinema.

'The King is clapped,' noted one Mass Observer, banally but accurately condensing the rationale of the British monarchy into a single sentence, 'not so much as a man, but as the symbol of the country.'

The King's daughters were crucial components of the symbolism – two mascots who embodied the tender values for which people believed that the war was being fought. As the girls had swept their Little Welsh House during the depression, now they 'did their bit' to beat Hitler, collecting tinfoil, rolling bandages and knitting socks. Both made contributions from their pocket money to the Red Cross, the Girl Guides and the Air Ambulance Fund, it was reported – which did not, on the face of it, leave them very much spare for sweets.

Official bulletins described the two girls as located 'somewhere in the country', to emphasise their similarity to so many other children dispatched from the inner cities and the perils of bombing. In fact, they were quite close to London, living at Windsor Castle, where they were able to see their parents who came down from Buckingham Palace most weekends. Crawfie was their mentor, and we owe to her a description of the 15th century Lancaster Tower where the girls were ensconced for the best part of five years, in their high and gloomy bedrooms carved out of the thick stone walls, with the wind whistling up and down the stone-flagged staircase.

'We seemed to live in a sort of underworld,' wrote the governess, describing the low-wattage light bulbs, the cabinets turned to the walls and the startling absence of the castle's priceless furniture and paintings which had been whisked off to distant rural hiding places for safe keeping.

A similarly remote destination was planned for the Princesses and their parents in the event of a German invasion. Their protection was in the care of the Coats Mission, an elite commando group named after its dashing leader Colonel Sir Jimmy Coats, who had a posse prepared to evacuate the girls, with room in their own armoured car for their nanny, their luggage – and one corgi. Elizabeth had been seven years old when her father gave her the first of these stumpy, bad-tempered little dogs, bred to round up Welsh sheep and cattle, and they had been her passion ever since.

Her other great animal passion was accelerated by a 1942 visit with her father to the Beckhampton stables in Wiltshire where the royal racehorses were stabled and trained. The King did not share the racing enthusiasms of his predecessors, but he had kept up the royal stables and the royal breeding studs for the sake of tradition and for the employment they provided – and he knew that his daughter loved horses. Elizabeth had been riding since her twelfth birthday when she started taking lessons from Horace Smith, the royal riding instructor to whom she made the much-quoted confession that 'had she not been who she was, she would like to be a lady living in the country with lots of horses and dogs.' Horseracing had not stopped in Britain because of the war, and in 1942 the royal stables had a highly fancied prospect for the Oaks and the Derby – Big Game, a three-year-old that had been bred at the royal studs. The Princess was allowed to go up and pat the magnificent animal, and she later admitted that she did not wash that hand for the rest of the day.

It was these years that saw the start of her fond and life-long friendship with her fellow horse enthusiast and later racing trainer, Henry Herbert, Lord Porchester – what else could his friends call him but 'Porchie'? He was one of a group of aristocratic young Guards officers who socialised with the Princesses in the middle and later stages of the war – the future Dukes of Buccleuch, Grafton and Rutland were also in the circle – and people with an eye for such things reckoned that these well-born young Englishmen represented her parents' 'First XI' of possible husbands for their elder daughter.

The courtships, such as they were, were decorous, open and hearty matters, involving scarcely more physical contact than hands on the hips for the occasional conga, and they developed in several cases into life-long friendships. Porchie (later Earl of Carnarvon), Hugh Euston (later Duke of Grafton) – a special favourite of George VI – and Johnny Dalkeith (later Duke of Buccleuch) became staples of Elizabeth's inner circle in later years. The conspicuous exception was Charles Manners, Duke of Rutland, said to be the only man to have got too fresh with the future Queen. He was quietly but firmly dropped from the team.

The entire concept of suitors or marriage candidates was totally academic from Elizabeth's point of view, however, since she already knew the young man whom she loved and wished to marry. She had made her choice – someone from inside the family, her third cousin just five years older than her, the dashing and fair-haired Royal Navy Lieutenant, Prince Philip of Greece: 'the man with whom,' according to Sir John Wheeler-Bennett in words later commissioned, read and approved by Elizabeth herself, 'Princess Elizabeth had been in love from their first meeting.'

There is some question as to when that first meeting might have been. Crawfie set the fateful moment in July 1939 at Dartmouth Naval College, when the thirteen-year-old Princess had spent an afternoon playing croquet with the eighteen-year-old midshipman in training for the war that was just weeks away: clearly bowled over herself, the governess thought Philip looked 'like a Viking'. But the cousins had met several times before that – at such family gatherings as the 1934 marriage of Elizabeth's uncle the Duke of Kent to Philip's cousin Princess Marina – and it was at Christmas 1943 that matters came to a head.

The festivities had started with a dance at Windsor Castle featuring the young aristocrats of the 'First XI', whose good behaviour and respect for their surroundings impressed the Queen. 'I fear they are starved of colour and beautiful things to look at in these days,' she wrote to her mother-in-law, Queen Mary. Prince Philip could not attend. He had been struck down with flu when he arrived on leave from his naval escort duties in the North Sea. But he was well enough to join the audience for the annual pantomime by the Windsor Great Park Primary School in which the two Princesses played starring roles – the 1943 choice of *Aladdin* providing the chance for such lines as 'Nip off to Nippon!' and other roundly applauded barbs at Japanese expense – and he stayed with the family over Christmas.

'We had a very gay time,' Princess Elizabeth related to Crawfie, 'with a film, dinner parties and dancing to the gramophone.'

The young couple 'frisked and capered away till near 1 am,' according to Tommy Lascelles who, as private secretary to the King, was keeping a beady eye on the practicalities to which he knew he would have to attend in the event of the romance developing – the 'matrimonial nigger in the woodpile,' as he later described it in his diary.

Old Queen Mary, Elizabeth's grandmother, was also watching closely. The couple had been 'in love for the last eighteen months, in fact longer I think,' she confided early in 1944 to her lady-in-waiting, the Countess of Airlie, and things had moved forward recently. Her Majesty had heard on the royal grapevine that the King of Greece was planning a formal approach on behalf of his energetic young cousin, and George VI confirmed the rumour.

He liked Philip, he told his mother: 'he is intelligent, has a good sense of humour and thinks about things in the right way.' But he and the Queen thought that at seventeen Elizabeth 'was too young for that now, as she has never met any young men of her own age.' There was also a convenient political excuse that Lascelles discovered as he investigated the practicalities of Philip, a Greek prince, taking British nationality. Neither the Greek nor British governments were keen to address the issue while a cloud hung over the Greek monarchy and its involvement with the pro-Nazi Metaxas regime.

Crawfie noticed a photograph of Philip on the Princess's mantelpiece.

'Is that altogether wise?' the governess asked. 'A number of people come and go.'

Since 1942 Elizabeth had been Colonel of the Grenadier Guards, receiving visitors on regimental business, and on her eighteenth birthday in 1944 she became a Counsellor of State, allowing her to deputise for her father if he were ill or abroad, and starting to take up her own public duties.

'You know what it will lead to,' said the governess. 'People will begin all sorts of gossip.'

'Oh dear, I suppose they will,' responded the Princess, and the picture vanished, to be replaced with another one showing Philip with a bushy beard that covered most of his features, yet hardly concealed his identity.

Elizabeth was not easily deflected from her purpose. At first glance the shy Princess and the dashing Viking played out a conventional stereotype – assertive male and submissive female. But as events unrolled, it was Elizabeth's quiet willpower and solid patience that won them both what they wanted. She accepted her parents' wish to stay officially non-committed; when the *New York Journal American* essayed British royal engagement predictions for the Princess in December 1943 they plumped for Hugh Euston and Charles Rutland.

Elizabeth meanwhile was looking for independence in other directions. In a war effort that was marked by social mobility, she and Margaret had been remarkably segregated from their contemporaries, and in the spring of 1945, with her nineteenth birthday approaching, she finally escaped to join the Auxiliary Territorial Service, or the 'Women's Army'

MECHANICAL TRAINING.
Second Subaltern Elizabeth Windsor joins the ATS vehicle maintenance course,
Aldershot. April 1945

as the ATS was generally known – 'No. 230873, Second Subaltern Elizabeth Alexandra Mary Windsor. Age: 18. Eyes: blue. Hair: brown. Height: 5 ft. 3 ins.' For a month she travelled to Aldershot every morning for a vehicle maintenance course, learning how to change tyres and cylinder heads, then returned to Windsor for dinner every evening to lecture her sister and parents on the joys of the internal combustion engine.

The Princess was wearing her khaki ATS uniform on the evening of 8th May 1945 when she appeared on the balcony of Buckingham Palace with her parents and Winston Churchill to acknowledge the cheering multitudes celebrating Victory in Europe day. Then she slipped away with some of the First XI (Philip was on active duty in the Far East) to mingle with the throngs in Whitehall and Piccadilly Circus, before gravitating back to the palace. There, for just once in her life, she became a face in the crowd like any other, looking up through the railings and shouting out in unison, 'We want the King!'

In September 1946, Buckingham Palace issued an official denial. Newspaper reports that Princess Elizabeth was engaged were untrue. The return of Prince Philip from Hong Kong to take up naval teaching duties in Britain had prompted the rumours, and the Palace was technically correct in denying them.

But only just. Since the spring of 1944 Elizabeth had obediently stuck by her parents' wish that she should not rush into a formal engagement, and in those two and a half years the politics of Philip's move to British citizenship had still not been resolved. Enough was enough. When the sub-lieutenant was granted a few weeks' leave from his teaching duties in the late summer of 1946, he came up to Balmoral to join the family's annual Scottish holiday and – in a picturesque spot in the hills, according to romantic legend – he formally proposed. Elizabeth did not hesitate. She had done her duty by father, mother, King, Queen and dithering governments. She would be twenty-one on her next birthday. She knew whom she loved and whom she wanted. She accepted Philip there and then.

It was not quite as simple as that, of course. Buckingham Palace had two priorities in the aftermath of victory – to thank the countries of the Empire for their support in the war and to restore the overtaxed health of the King – and the two objectives were neatly combined in a family tour to South Africa scheduled for the spring of 1947. Plans were already in hand for a formal celebration of Elizabeth's coming of age that would occur in South Africa, and the King did not see how the announcement of her engagement could neatly or properly be made before that.

By now it was clear that the nervous and debilitated George VI was doing everything he could to avoid losing his elder daughter to another man, and Elizabeth humoured him yet again. She and Philip agreed to wait until after South Africa, but that October they both attended the wedding of Lord Mountbatten's daughter Patricia in the parish church of Romsey in Hampshire, and their attraction to each other was plain to see.

'When I come back,' said Elizabeth to her grandmother's old friend, Lady Airlie, thanking her for an early twenty-first birthday present, 'we will have a celebration – maybe two celebrations.'

The tour proved to be Elizabeth's triumph, the high spot arriving on the evening of 21st April 1947 with her coming-of-age broadcast of dedication:

I declare before you all that my whole life, whether it be long or short, shall be devoted to your service and the service of our great Imperial Commonwealth to which we all belong. But I shall not have strength to carry out this resolution unless you join in it with me, as I now invite you to do; I know that your support will be unfailingly given. God help me to make good my vow; and God bless all of you who are willing to share in it.

'Perfect,' declared Queen Mary, listening to the broadcast in London and dispatching an instant letter of congratulation, '… and, of course, I wept.'

PRIVATE UNDERSTANDING.

Lieutenant Philip Mountbatten, 25, and Princess Elizabeth, 20, at the wedding of Lord Mountbatten's daughter Patricia in Romsey, Hampshire. October 1946

The broadcast was as total and elegant a statement of the modern monarchical ideal as words could encapsulate, and the words were the work of the archetypal royal servant, Tommy Lascelles, whose own summing up of the tour gave pride of place to Elizabeth:

> She has come on in the most surprising way, and all in the right direction ... When necessary, she can take on the old bores with much of her mother's skill, and never spares herself in that exhausting part of royal duty. For a child of her years, she has got an astonishing solicitude for other people's comfort.

This thought and consideration for the convenience of others, noted the Private Secretary, who had served George V, Edward VIII and George VI, not to mention Queen

Mary and the apparently charming Queen Elizabeth, 'is not a normal characteristic of that family.'

Lascelles particularly admired Elizabeth's surprising willingness to stand up to her parents:

> She has developed an admirable technique of going up behind her mother and prodding her in the Achilles tendon with the point of her umbrella when time is being wasted in unnecessary conversation. And when necessary – not infrequently – she tells her father off to rights.

Princess Elizabeth had come of age in no mistake. She was ready – and she needed to be.

DECK GAMES.
Princess Elizabeth relaxes with the officers of HMS Vanguard *on the royal tour to South Africa. April 1947*

2

A delighted sort of family feeling
1947–1953

When George VI returned from his 1947 tour of South Africa, he was looking and feeling terrible. In his twelve weeks away he had lost seventeen pounds in weight. Eighteen months later his doctors would diagnose arteriosclerosis and eventually lung cancer, but his immediate symptom was a peppery temper that was fiercer than ever – and an obstinate refusal to accept that the time had finally come for his daughter to marry Philip.

The Queen shared her husband's continuing doubts – particularly about Philip's politics. Shortly before the tour, the young man had got involved in 'a rather heated discussion' with the ultra-conservative Queen and subsequently wrote to apologise if he had said 'anything I ought not to have said.' He hoped she did not think him 'violently argumentative and an exponent of socialism.'

That was, in fact, exactly what the future Queen Mother did think of Philip then – and almost certainly for the rest of her life. He was a well-meaning but erratic progressive, in her view, like his ambitious and interfering uncle, Dickie Mountbatten. '[Philip] is untried as yet,' she wrote in a heart-searching letter about her daughter's feelings that she drafted then decided not to send to Tommy Lascelles. 'One can only pray that she has made the right decision.'

Elizabeth and Philip, for their parts, were more in love and more determined than ever. They had written to each other constantly while the Princess was travelling – the separation that was intended to test them had brought them still closer – and Philip had taken the question of his naturalisation into his own hands. He had secured British citizenship, as he was entitled to through his service in the Royal Navy, jettisoning his Greek royal title and taking the anglicised surname of his uncle. No longer a foreign prince of complicated origins, he was now plain Lieutenant Philip Mountbatten RN.

The previous September, Philip had written effusively to the Queen about his feelings for her daughter: 'I am sure I do not deserve all the good things that have happened to me. To have been spared in the war and seen victory, to have been given the chance to rest and re-adjust myself, to have fallen in love, completely and unreservedly ...' With the end of the tour, he renewed the campaign. He was quite sure that the South Africa delay had been right, he wrote emolliently to his would-be mother-in-law early in June 1947, but now he and the Princess wanted to start their new life together.

Elizabeth's personal conviction was the decisive factor. Whatever her parents' doubts, she herself had none, and she was now twenty-one – an adult who declined to accept further delay. She had 'made up her mind', she made clear to her mother and father. She was finding her public duties painful as curious crowds shouted out 'Where's Philip?' The dutiful daughter finally put her foot down and, faced with her resolve, her parents bowed to the inevitable.

'She has known him ever since she was 12,' wrote the still-worried Queen on 7th July 1947 to her sister May *very secretly* (underlined in black and red). 'I think she is *really* fond of him, and I do pray that she will be very happy.'

Three days later, the secret was revealed.

'It is with the greatest pleasure,' read a statement from Buckingham Palace, 'that the King and Queen announce the betrothal of their dearly beloved daughter the Princess Elizabeth to Lieutenant Philip Mountbatten RN ... to which union the King has gladly given his consent.'

'They both came to see me after luncheon looking radiant,' wrote a delighted Queen Mary, who gave her granddaughter some family jewellery. Her lady-in-waiting Mabell Airlie was impressed by how Philip's costume reflected the country's current state of 'austerity': 'his uniform was shabby – the usual "after-the-war" look ... I liked him for not having got a new one for the occasion, as many men would have done, to make an impression.'

Life was tough in post-war Britain. Clothing, like food, could only be purchased with coupons from a government-issued ration book, and the officially-encouraged atmosphere of make-do-and mend raised tricky questions about the proper scale of the forthcoming royal wedding.

'I think it is a damn waste of money,' declared one lower-middle class woman of thirty, interviewed by Mass-Observation. 'I don't see why she should have everything when there are so many who have to make do with makeshift weddings and others can't get married at all because they have no home to go to.'

Mass-Obs conducted a straw poll that showed that while 37 per cent of those interviewed looked forward to a grand royal wedding, 36 per cent considered it an extravagance (10 per cent voted 'Let her alone'). For Princess Elizabeth, sharing her joy with the nation meant sharing its grumbling as well. A group of left-wing MPs lodged a formal protest at royal spending in such a time of national distress, and the Labour Prime Minister, Clement Attlee, felt he had to write to the Palace about the possibly unpatriotic origins of the 'Lyons silk' reportedly stitched into the bride's wedding dress.

'The *wedding dress*,' replied Tommy Lascelles, scarcely bothering to conceal his sarcasm, 'contains silk from Chinese silk worms, but woven in Scotland and Kent. The *wedding train* contains silk produced by Kentish silk worms and woven in London. The *going-away dress* contains 4 or 5 yards of Lyons silk which was not specially imported but was part of the stock held by the dressmaker [Norman Hartnell] under permit.'

ROYAL WEDDING.
Princess Elizabeth and Lieutenant Philip Mountbatten leave Westminster Abbey.
20ᵗʰ November 1947

Hartnell himself later joined in to point out that while some of the silk worms might be Chinese, they were *Nationalist* silkworms, not Communist – and when the controversy attained the status of full cabinet discussion, it was Aneurin Bevan, the bluff heart and conscience of Labour's left wing, who finally restored a sense of proportion.

'As long as we have a monarchy,' he declared, 'the monarchy's work has got to be done well.'

That proved to be the national consensus by the time the wedding day rolled round on 20th November 1947. The list of over 1,500 wedding gifts displayed extraordinary generosity by ordinary members of the public – particularly when it came to the most coveted feminine asset of the times:

> 351. Mrs David Mudd. A pair of nylon stockings.
>
> 352. Miss Ethel Newcombe. A piece of old lace.
>
> 353. Mrs E. Klarood. A pair of nylon stockings.

'The feeling is genuine enough,' wrote a female Mass Observer from Leatherhead in Surrey. 'A delighted sort of family feeling. I always get it when watching any Royal Do.'

The family themselves had also sorted out their feelings.

'I was so proud of you and thrilled at having you so close to me on our long walk in Westminster Abbey,' wrote the King to his daughter a few days after the ceremony. 'But when I handed your hand to the Archbishop, I felt that I had lost something very precious.'

George VI now felt guilty about the delay he had imposed.

'I was rather afraid that you had thought I was being hard-hearted about it. I was so anxious for you to come to South Africa, as you know. Our family, us four, the "Royal Family", must remain together – with additions, of course, at suitable moments!'

All was forgiven so far as Elizabeth was concerned.

'Darling Mummy,' she wrote on the second day of her honeymoon at the Mountbatten estate at Broadlands, Hampshire, 'I don't know where to begin this letter, or what to say, but I know I must write it somehow because I feel so much about it. First of all, to say thank you ... I think I've got the best mother and father in the world, and I only hope that I can bring up my children in the happy atmosphere of love and fairness which Margaret and I have grown up in.'

The Queen loved this letter, re-reading it many times, she told the Princess – 'and each time I feel more grateful for our darling little daughter!'

The arrival of a healthy son and heir within less than a year completed the family and the national joy. Prince Charles was born on 14th November 1948, and Princess Anne was born less than two years later – 'heavenly little creatures' according to their doting grandmother: 'I can't tell you what a difference it makes having [them] in the house ... They cheer us up more than I can say.'

The reason why the baby prince and princess were staying in their grandparents' 'house' (Royal Lodge, Windsor – it was early April 1951) was because their mother was abroad enjoying an interlude unlike any other in her life, the closest she would ever come to everyday existence. Philip's naval career, which both he and the Palace felt he should keep pursuing, had taken him to Malta on active service with command of a ship of his own, and Elizabeth went along too – she was the captain's wife. For three spells that added up to nearly a year she was able to do relatively ordinary things like swim off a beach, drive her own car, visit a hairdressing salon and do her own shopping with real money in her handbag. These were the months when she learned to stand on the sideline chatting to other officers' wives and pretending to look *really interested* while their husbands tore around the field playing polo.

But the King's worsening health imposed another reality. King George VI was never told that he had cancer, but in May 1951 his doctors handed him over to the care of a chest surgeon who prescribed the removal of a lung for reasons of 'bronchial blockage'. In July Lieutenant-Commander Philip Mountbatten left the Royal Navy on indefinite leave, to be sworn in later that year as a member of the Privy Council, along with his wife, who was assuming more and more duties for her father. When Elizabeth set off with Philip on the last day of January 1952 on the long southern hemisphere tour that the King had been due to carry out, her Private Secretary, Martin Charteris, carried sealed envelopes containing a draft Accession Declaration and a message to both Houses of Parliament.

The tour was another 'thank you' to Commonwealth countries – in this case to the East African colonies, Australia and New Zealand – for their help in the war, and it started in Kenya where, on 5th February 1952, Elizabeth and her husband travelled to Treetops, the famous tree house overlooking a waterhole where animals came after sunset. It was in this curious situation, up in the branches of a fig tree watching wildlife, that Princess Elizabeth became Queen Elizabeth II in the early hours of 6th February 1952, for sometime that night at Sandringham in Norfolk, after a happy day of shooting across the East Anglia countryside, her father George VI died of a thrombosis in his sleep.

Alerted by aides, her husband had to break the news to her.

'He took her up to the garden of the lodge where they were staying,' remembered Philip's Private Secretary, Michael Parker. 'And they walked slowly up and down the lawn while he talked and talked and talked to her.'

Elizabeth II's response to her father's death was remarkably controlled.

'She was sitting erect, fully accepting her destiny,' remembered Martin Charteris of the moment he went to

NEW QUEEN.
Elizabeth II arrives at London Airport from Kenya on 7ᵗʰ February 1952, the day after the death of her father George VI

discuss the practicalities of cancelling the tour and reorganising as soon as possible for the 4,000 mile journey home.

Philip's valet John Dean watched the new Queen leave her seat once or twice on the long flight back to London and thought she looked as if she had been crying. But no one saw any tears. When she emerged from the plane at London Airport on 7th February 1952, she was a small, composed figure in black whose appearance at the top of the steps was massively important and somehow comforting – the first of several occasions when the emotional calm and solidity of Elizabeth II would provide relief to an overwrought nation.

'When I heard first of all,' said a forty-five-year-old carpenter, talking of the death of George VI, 'I felt it was a personal loss, as though some of my own people had died.'

'My husband poured himself out a brandy,' recalled another contributor to Mass-Observation, 'and I said "Pour one out for me."... It was such a shock. All I can say is, thank goodness we've still got Churchill.'

After six years of Labour government, the wartime hero had recently been re-elected with a slender majority, and he was in tears himself as he drove back from the airport welcome ceremony, dictating the text of his radio broadcast that night.

'The King,' he declared, had 'walked with death, as if death were a companion he did not fear ... In the end death came as a friend, and after a happy day of sunshine and sport ... he fell asleep as every man or woman who strives to fear God and nothing else in the world may hope to do.'

Now, said the Prime Minister (born 1874), the 'Second Queen Elizabeth' was ascending the throne at the same age as the first, nearly 400 years earlier, and 'I, whose youth was passed in the august, unchallenged and tranquil glories of the Victorian era, may well feel a thrill in invoking, once more, the prayer and anthem,"God Save the Queen!"'

The theme of a second Elizabethan Age became the relentless signature tune of the months that followed. 'The Signs Are Bright for a Great Revival' promised articles by learned historians, and the *Daily Express* presented its readers with a tableau of 'modern Elizabethans' with ballerina Margot Fonteyn in farthingale, Sir Frank Whittle (inventor of the jet engine) in doublet and hose and the poet

T.S. Eliot (born an American) wearing a ruff. Five faces were left blank, and readers were invited to nominate who they thought would inspire the new renaissance.

The crowning of the new Elizabeth was set for 2nd June 1953, the day estimated by meteorologists to be the likeliest to produce sunshine the following summer – which gave a full sixteen months to transport the contingents of troops from around the Empire who would parade the streets in the style of the century's three previous coronations (Edward VII and Georges V and VI). The Ministry of Works turned central London into a ceremonial theme park – this queen must be crowned in the sight of all the people – with processional arches and long, covered stands that gave the Mall and Whitehall the appearance of a race track. Every seat in the stands was sold the day booking opened – tickets were selling on the black market for as much as £40 or £50 each (£900–£1,100 today) – and the capital, like every British city, town and village, was decked out with flags and bunting for months ahead. The Cold War was in full swing, and visitors to Russia came back ridiculing the cult of personality surrounding Stalin, but that was nothing compared to Britain's home-grown profusion of posters and souvenirs, from tin pots to tea towels, emblazoned with the solemn, dark-eyed likeness of Elizabeth.

The enigmatic young woman at the heart of this hysteria remained reserved and shy – too shy, in fact. When presented with the proposal that her coronation ceremony should be shared with the 1.5 million of her subjects who owned the recently-developed television sets, Elizabeth said no. There were certain moments of the ceremony, like the anointing with sacred oil of the bared upper part of her chest, which she wished to keep private. But more deeply she shared the view of her family and courtiers – the 'Telly' was just impossibly 'common'. She did not need to be crowned in the sight of all *those* people.

3

New Elizabethans
1953–1969

When the mobs rush forward in the Mall they are taking part in the last circus of a civilization that has lost faith in itself, and sold itself for a splendid triviality ... My objection to the Royalty symbol is that it is dead; it is the gold filling in a mouthful of decay ... It distresses me that there should be so many empty minds, so many empty lives in Britain to sustain this fatuous industry.

John Osborne, *October 1957*

As the newly crowned Queen Elizabeth II moved out of Westminster Abbey at the end of her Coronation on 2nd June 1953, her sister Princess Margaret reached out playfully to brush a piece of fluff from the uniform of the handsome comptroller of her widowed mother's new household, Group Captain Peter Townsend, DSO, DFC. The Princess ran her white-gloved hand along the medals above his breast pocket with a flirtatiousness that caught the eye of a watching journalist, and with that gesture, the royal story slipped sharply off the glorious high road of pageantry and cheering. Britain took down the bunting and declared open season on the monarchy.

Shortly before the Coronation an intellectual young aristocrat, John Grigg, Lord Altrincham, had written an article complaining at the non-representative makeup of the congregation in Westminster Abbey. Every single peer, down to the most obscure, had been allotted a place, he noted, but that left less than 100 seats for the 625 elected members of Parliament – the true representatives of the people – who were submitted to the indignity of drawing lots for a 1-in-6 chance of getting inside. Nor did the small number of non-white faces in the pews begin to reflect the multi-racial make-up of the colonies and Commonwealth nations of Africa, India and the Caribbean to whose headship Elizabeth II was being crowned.

Altrincham's complaints were ignored in the frenzy of Coronation fever, but four years later he returned to the fray in a special issue of the *National and English Review*, a small circulation journal of ideas that he owned and edited. Though he claimed that his criticisms were aimed at Her Majesty's 'tweedy' advisors, his comments were a scarcely camouflaged attack upon Elizabeth herself. Her speeches were 'prim little sermons', he wrote. Her speaking style was 'a pain in the neck', and the overall impression was of 'a priggish schoolgirl, captain of the hockey team, a prefect and a recent candidate for confirmation ... Like her mother, she appears to be unable to string even a few sentences together without a written text.'

After a furore of angry editorials the *Daily Mail* discovered, to its horror, that a majority of 16-to-34-year-olds actually agreed with Altrincham's criticisms, and that a majority of all age groups thought (by a ratio of 55:21) that the Court circle around Elizabeth II should be widened. On 6th August 1957 a member of the League of Empire Loyalists stepped up to Altrincham as he was leaving Television House and slapped him hard across the face, provoking another round of headlines.

The most significant aspect of the attack was that it took place outside the headquarters of the recently established Independent Television News. The BBC had loyally suppressed all mention of Altrincham and his views, nannying the monarchy and doing its duty as a pillar of the establishment in the style of its famous royal commentator

TAKE THAT!

Mr B.K. Burbage expresses the outrage of loyal Britons at what Lord Altrincham had written about their Queen. 6ᵗʰ August 1957

Richard Dimbleby, while the new ITV, featuring Britain's first female newsreader, Barbara Mandell, gave the rebel peer airtime and a soapbox – and had not been shy in reporting the romantic dilemma of the Queen's younger sister. Margaret's group captain was a thrice-decorated Battle of Britain Hurricane pilot hero, but he was also 'a divorcé' and, though he had not been the 'guilty party' (he had sued his wife for *her* adultery), to the Palace establishment, it was Edward and Wallis all over again.

'You must be either mad or bad,' Tommy Lascelles famously declared when Peter Townsend went to confide in the Private Secretary that he and the Princess 'were deeply in love with each other and wished to get married.' The Royal Marriages Act (devised in 1772 to regulate the scandalous marital arrangements of the Hanoverians) denied Margaret, then 22, the right to marry without government consent before her twenty-fifth birthday and without Parliamentary consent thereafter.

Elizabeth was more sympathetic. She had known the pain of love denied – and, like her mother, she was particularly fond of the sensitive Townsend, who had done wonders in soothing the 'gnashes' of George VI in his later years. She invited the couple to the palace to talk the problem through over a quiet dinner with Philip – there was a touching symmetry between the two sisters and their handsome war hero partners, with Elizabeth displaying, according to Townsend, a 'movingly simple and sympathetic acceptance of her sister's love for me.'

Elizabeth wanted her sister to be happy, and it was eventually decided that Townsend should go into temporary exile until the summer of 1955 when Margaret would become twenty-five. A job was quickly found for him as air attaché to the British embassy in Brussels.

But the fallacy in the well-meaning compromise was that, aged twenty-five, thirty or sixty-five, Margaret would always need government consent for a relationship that involved public approval and public funds, and two months after Margaret's twenty-fifth birthday, at the end of October 1955, Sir Anthony Eden, Conservative Prime Minister since Churchill's retirement six months earlier, brought the Queen the bad news. His cabinet could not recommend that taxpayers' money should go to support the upkeep of

FOND FAREWELL.

Sir Winston Churchill dressed as a Garter knight for his retirement dinner at Downing Street on 4th April 1955

the Princess and the divorced group captain. Nor, he added, would they push for Parliamentary approval of the marriage unless Margaret renounced her rights to the throne.

Margaret surrendered immediately – ceasing to be a princess was not on her agenda. She and Peter decided 'at exactly the same second ...' she told friends privately. '*That* was it – we did it together.' To the general public, she spared the personal details and explained her decision to renounce Townsend in religious terms – she was 'mindful,' she said, 'of the Church's teaching that Christian marriage is indissoluble.'

'What a wonderful person the Holy Spirit is!' exclaimed the Archbishop of Canterbury when the Princess told him the news, and the world in general preferred to accept that Margaret's decision was based on high-minded and selfless spiritual motives rather than on the depressingly material prospect, as the writer Kenneth Rose put it, of 'life in a cottage on a group captain's salary.'

In later years, however, the Princess would admit to baser feelings whenever she encountered her sister's Private Secretary, Tommy Lascelles, who had tried to sabotage the love match from the start, she felt, and who failed to make clear to herself or to her sister Elizabeth the futility of waiting for two more painful years. After she married Anthony Armstrong Jones, Lord Snowdon, in 1960, Margaret went to live in Kensington Palace and discovered that Lascelles, long retired, was her neighbour in the warren of apartments there. She did her best to stay away from her old adversary, but she would encounter his stooped frame from time to time, trudging across the courtyard in front of her car, and as she looked through the windscreen, she confessed to friends, she found it difficult not to command her chauffeur to step on the accelerator and crunch the old courtier into the gravel.

Sir Anthony Eden, the handsome, matinee idol Prime Minister whose cabinet effectively scuppered the romance of Margaret and Peter Townsend, was himself a divorcé who had remarried. But he lacked the courage to cross swords with his more conventional colleagues – and this cowardice characterised his short-lived premiership.

Eden's 1956 invasion of Egypt to recapture the Suez Canal in collusion with France and Israel ended abruptly when America ordered all three nations home, shattering Britain's post-war illusions of global might. It later became clear that Eden must have lied to the Queen when he presented her with the same false scenario he offered to his cabinet and to Parliament – that France and Britain felt compelled to intervene as honest brokers after Israel invaded Egypt without their knowledge. In fact, ministers of the three nations had concocted the whole sequence of events a week earlier at a secret meeting in the Parisian suburb of Sèvres – the so-called Sèvres Protocol of which the embarrassing details were published twenty years later.

Eden saddled his monarch with more direct embarrassment, however, when he collapsed under the pressure of events early in 1957, leaving her to select a new prime minister. In practice this was the job of the majority party, the Conservatives, who had no leadership election process,* but had two strong candidates in Harold MacMillan, the Chancellor of the Exchequer, and R.A. 'Rab' Butler, who had been serving as Eden's deputy during the crisis. A confidential sounding of the party's Westminster MPs showed a clear majority for MacMillan, and the Cabinet delivered the same verdict when Lord Salisbury, the long-serving Conservative elder statesman who could not pronounce his 'r's, called in the ministers one by one to ask whether they opted for 'Wab' or 'Hawold'. The Hawolds had it – there was quite a surprising consensus for the Chancellor.

But this was not the result that the media had been predicting. On the morning of Thursday 10th January 1957 every British newspaper – except *The Times*, which was non-committal – had plumped for Butler, the quieter, less 'old school' candidate (he had been to Marlborough and Cambridge, not Eton and Oxford). So when MacMillan was summoned to the palace at 2.00 pm and invited to form a government, the cry of 'Fix!' went up. Writing in *The Spectator* two years earlier, Henry Fairlie had identified an upper-class English matrix of social influence and political string-pulling that he called 'The Establishment', and here they were in action – grouse-shooting Old Etonians every one, from Salisbury, Eden and MacMillan to Michael Adeane, Tommy Lascelles' stuffier-than-stuffy successor as Royal Private Secretary. Butler

---

* The Parliamentary Labour Party had been electing its leaders since 1906.

FORMAL ADDRESS.
Elizabeth II delivers her traditional Christmas Day broadcast from Government House, Auckland, while visiting New Zealand in 1954

quite enjoyed the grouse moor, in fact, but had a withered hand that made it impossible for him to shoot.

In 1957 most critics gave the young Queen a pass under the pressure of events, particularly as 'Supermac' became a curiously effective and entertaining prime minister, coaxing Britain out of its post-Suez depression and winning re-election in 1959 with a brash appeal to consumer spending power – 'You've never had it so good.' But when scandal and illness forced his resignation in 1963, Elizabeth found herself entangled once again in the vague and mystical Tory rituals of 'emergence' and 'soundings'.

The scandal involved MacMillan's Secretary for War, Jack Profumo, who had an affair with Christine Keeler, a call-girl and reputed mistress of a Russian spy, and then lied about it. MacMillan was curiously dilatory in pursuing the affair, which involved a society osteopath, Stephen Ward, and high jinks at Cliveden, the grand Thames Valley mansion of Lord

Astor. Here was the charmed circle at work again, and they seemed even more in evidence a few months later when a prostate operation laid MacMillan low. Despite being in his hospital bed and on his way out as prime minister, MacMillan insisted on conducting his own 'soundings' of the party and handed the Queen, who went to visit him in hospital, his resignation and a memorandum recommending his successor: his Foreign Secretary, the Old Etonian 14th Earl of Home.

Once again the outcome of the undefined Tory 'emergence' process defied public and press expectations. The Conservative constituency associations had not even known that the charming but laughably aristocratic Home was in the running. The 14th Earl (who had once played cricket for Middlesex) was MacMillan's personal compromise candidate in a field that, as in 1957, featured R.A. Butler, whom MacMillan seemed determined to exclude at all costs. It was difficult not to suspect foul play, and several mistakes on the part of Elizabeth made both the Crown and herself seem complicit in the ailing premier's manoeuvres.

The basic problem was that the Queen knew and liked 'Alec' – she met him frequently on the grouse moor. He was no wild card to her or to Michael Adeane, her Private Secretary, and neither she nor the blinkered courtier took on board how it looked to the world for her to go to MacMillan's hospital bedside, a gesture that was human but by no means monarchical, then invite a backwoods peer to the palace a few hours later.

In fact, on MacMillan's advice, Elizabeth only invited the 14th Earl to *see* if he could form a government, and if Butler had not accepted Home's invitation to serve as his Foreign Secretary, then Butler himself would probably have become prime minister. But this constitutional distinction failed to impress most people. The Queen should have kept the Crown aloof from the fray, it became clear, sending her private secretary to the hospital then instructing the

Conservative party to do its own horse-trading and present the Palace with the name of its undisputed candidate. Once MacMillan had resigned, his 'soundings' memorandum was without constitutional status and should have been ignored – a British prime minister has no right to pick his own successor, let alone harness the Crown to his scheming.

It was the low point in Elizabeth's constitutional care of her office. Her reliance on a small, upper crust circle of her own sort had betrayed her grandfather's carefully constructed alliance of throne and people against the upper classes, confirming the refrain of Lord Altrincham, John Osborne and the 'Angry Young Men' of the 1950s. The collusion of Crown and establishment would similarly infuse the theme songs of their successors – the socially-questioning pop musicians and satirists of the 'Swinging Sixties'.

> *Sexual intercourse began*
> *In nineteen sixty-three*
> *(Which was rather late for me) –*
> *Between the end of the Chatterley ban*
> *And the Beatles' first LP.*
>
> Philip Larkin, *'Annus Mirabilis'*

Decades do not always start on time. The sixties took a little time to get swinging – and if 1963 was the year when the earth started to move for the poet-librarian Philip Larkin in Hull, it was also the year when the scorn prompted by the Profumo and Tory succession scandals started to impact the monarchy. Just ten years after the loyalist hysteria of the Coronation, the BBC's late night satirical show, *That Was The Week That Was*, depicted the royal barge sinking – with the Royal Family on board. As the band played the national anthem, a Dimbleby-like commentator intoned, 'and now the Queen, smiling radiantly, is swimming for her life. Her Majesty is wearing a silk ensemble in canary yellow ... Perhaps the lip readers among you can make out what Prince Philip, Duke of Edinburgh, is saying to the captain of the barge as she sinks.'

In political terms the decade began the following year with the arrival of a Labour government under a nimble, pipe-smoking statistician and economist who had won his place at Oxford from grammar schools in Cheshire and Huddersfield – 'the 14th Mr Wilson', as Alec Douglas-Home gracefully dubbed his victorious opponent in the general election of October 1964. Harold Wilson promised to transform Britain with the 'white heat' of scientific and technological change, and his two spells in power initiated some startling social shake-ups: divorce law reform; the liberalisation of censorship, homosexuality, immigration and abortion; the beginning of decimal coinage (farewell to the farthing and florin); the founding of the Open University for students of all ages; and the abolition of capital punishment. Abroad, he withdrew from Britain's military commitments east of Suez and, unlike his successors in both parties, he also kept Britain out of America's imperial wars, rebuffing US pressure to send British troops to Vietnam.

Elizabeth and Wilson got off to a prickly start when the new Prime Minister seemed inattentive to royal conventions, bringing his wife along for the ceremony of kissing hands – his formal appointment as prime minister – plus his father, his sister, his two sons and his personal secretary, Marcia Williams. The assembled spectators were disappointed to discover that no actual kissing took place – the actual application of the prime ministerial lip to the royal hand was taken 'as read'.

More seriously, Wilson had assumed that his weekly meeting with the monarch would take the form of a cosy round-up of the political scene, and had not appreciated the meticulous care that Elizabeth devoted to her reading of 'the boxes', the battered, red-dyed rams' leather dispatch boxes[†]

[†] The boxes are built of wood and lined with lead – originally to ensure the box sank if thrown overboard in the event of capture. Today they are designed to be bomb-proof.

of Cabinet and Foreign Office documents brought to her every day (except Christmas Day and Easter Sunday) for her perusal and sometimes signature.

'Very interesting,' she remarked at an early audience, 'this idea of a new town in the Bletchley area.'

The Prime Minister looked blank. It was the first he had heard of the proposal to build the Buckinghamshire new town that would become famous as Milton Keynes – a plan set out in a Cabinet Committee paper which Wilson had planned to read later.

'I shall certainly advise my successor to do his homework before his Audience,' he said a dozen years later in his retirement speech, 'and to read all his telegrams and the Cabinet Committee papers in time, and not leave them to the weekend, or he will feel like an unprepared schoolboy.'

From this shaky beginning, an unexpected partnership developed. Elizabeth appreciated the intelligence of a man who had become an Oxford don at the age of twenty-one, and who also took an interest in her own recent 'new' family – her younger sons Andrew and Edward had been born in 1960 and 1964. Wilson, for his part, was warmed by Elizabeth's quite feminine concern when he was stressed and tired, and by the feeling of absolute support that she radiated. The Queen was the one working colleague, he confided to the Irish Prime Minister, to whom he could take his problems without feeling he might be sharpening a knife for his own back.

She also worked hard at getting along with some of Wilson's more left-wing colleagues, like his Postmaster General, Anthony Wedgwood-Benn, who had a plan to modernise the mail by producing large pictorial issues after the style of the banana republics – and to take the Queen's head off British stamps altogether. Elizabeth appeared to show great interest when Benn laid out his first set of headless designs on the palace carpet.

'Did she get down on the floor with you?' enquired Wilson with envy when Benn recounted the story to him later.

But Elizabeth did not, in fact, kneel on the carpet beside her republican Postmaster General, and though Benn did eventually manage to shrink the royal profile to a token (and rather elegant) silhouette in the corner of commemorative issues, the Queen fought a rearguard action through her private secretaries that eventually compelled him to admit defeat.

'The plain fact is, I shan't get the Queen's head off the stamps,' noted the republican plaintively in his diary in December 1965. 'And it is probably rather foolish of me to go on knocking my head against a brick wall.'

Benn failed to appreciate how the essence of Elizabeth's job was the concealing of her personal feelings – her talent and also, on occasions, her Achilles heel, as in October 1966 when a mountainous coal tip collapsed on the Welsh mining village of Aberfan, engulfing the local primary school, killing 116 children and 28 adults. So shocking was the tragedy that Elizabeth felt this was one occasion when she would *not* be able to master her distress – and when her presence would, in any case, hamper the rescue work.

'People will be looking after *me*,' she objected when her advisors urged her to make the journey to South Wales. 'So perhaps they'll miss some poor child that might have been found under the wreckage.'

Extending personal comfort and softness was not something that the Queen did very well in her personal life, and she found it still harder in public – she actually felt unqualified for the heavy responsibility of ministering to people's sorrow.

'She has no vanity ...' said one of the aides at the daily meetings that tried to get her to budge. 'She simply has no sense or instinct for the balm her presence brings.'

In the end, the Queen *did* make the journey to Aberfan, eight days after the coal tip had collapsed when rescue efforts had been abandoned. Her gaunt features, etched with grief, were the more moving for being so clearly genuine – and

FACE OF GRIEF.
The Queen visits the Welsh village of Aberfan following the fatal collapse of a coal tip on the local school. 30ᵗʰ October 1966

unlike many public figures who rushed down ahead of her in 1966, she has also been back in the years since then to revisit the village and talk again with the survivors. Twice.

Buckingham Palace press and public relations in the 1950s had been in the hands of Commander Richard Colville, a snooty and unhelpful naval officer who made a worthy companion to Tommy Lascelles and Michael Adeane. With a mouth that turned down at both corners, Colville was known inside the palace as 'Sunshine', and as 'the abominable No-man' to Fleet Street's royal correspondents who had to struggle daily with his disdain.

'He was an anti-Press Secretary,' recalled Martin Charteris, Colville's palace colleague for many years.

The Queen let the commander's career run its course – she was not a good sacker. But as the sixties started to swing, she brought in some fresh talent. William 'Bill' Heseltine was a polished young western Australian who had been private secretary to Robert Menzies, Australia's longest-serving (and highly pro-British) prime minister.

'I've never had anything to do with the press,' objected Heseltine when first offered the London job.

'They'll probably consider that rather an advantage,' was the dry response of his Canberra recruiting officer.

The effect was instantaneous.

'Bill had such an easy manner with the Queen,' remembers one of the party on a royal tour to South America. 'He would come up from the back of the plane and plonk himself down to go through the newspapers with her. It was very natural and casual – never disrespectful.'

'There is a distinct wind of change at the Palace,' recorded a perceptibly astonished BBC memorandum in 1968, the year of Colville's retirement. The new Press Secretary had come to the broadcaster with the idea that was to catapult royal public relations into a new era – the landmark documentary film that was eventually titled *Royal Family*.

Heseltine had been besieged with press proposals to mark Prince Charles's coming of age the following year, and it occurred to the Australian that, rather than disrupt the young man's studies at Cambridge and the Welsh University of Aberystwyth, it would make more sense to depict the life and work that lay ahead of the Prince – the day-to-day life of a family-based constitutional sovereign. This turned out to fit precisely with an idea that Elizabeth had been discussing with John Brabourne, the film producer son-in-law of Lord Mountbatten.

Brabourne had just produced *The Life and Times of Lord Mountbatten*, the TV hit that rivalled the earlier success of *The Forsyte Saga* as a weekly attraction that kept Britain's middle class at home for the night. Elizabeth would not miss an episode – she called it 'Dickie time'. So when Brabourne proposed that she should be the subject of his follow-up film, she proved receptive.

'Will we have some say?' she asked.

In the event, a Palace committee headed by Prince Philip had total say, with Heseltine functioning as the on-line producer to Richard Cawston, the documentary filmmaker recruited by Brabourne. The BBC shot more than 40 hours of footage for the 90 carefully edited minutes that eventually appeared on the screen, and Heseltine made sure there were no grouse moor or pheasant-shooting sequences; the many hours spent by the Royal Family blasting little birds out of the sky did not match the desired image of middle class normalcy. Prince Philip wanted to excise the sequence that showed the four-year-old Prince Edward bursting into tears when the string on a cello being played by Prince Charles snapped suddenly and hurt him.

'Prince Philip thought it was unkind to little Ed,' recalled one of the production team. 'But in the end he was persuaded that the tears added to the authenticity.'

Authenticity – or at least the appearance of it – made *Royal Family* a sensation, a TV landmark to rival the Coronation, when it was released in June 1969. Viewed in more than 125 countries, including twice, coast-to-coast, at peak time in the USA, the film was seen by more people than any other documentary ever made. Viewers could not get enough of the Royal Family as they grilled sausages on a barbecue, gossiped with each other, or, wonder of wonders, even sat down together to watch television. Elizabeth herself was the surprise and the star of what was, essentially, a glorified home movie: she came across as the relaxed and rather playful person that she usually was in private.

NEW FAMILY.
Prince Charles, 20, gives his five-year-old brother Edward a ride in a go-kart at Windsor. 15th May 1969

The following month came another triumph – the investiture of her son Charles as Prince of Wales at Caernarfon Castle. The pseudo-medieval pageant was as bogus as the acrylic canopy that Lord Snowdon devised to keep off the rain. All Princes of Wales were invested in England until 1911 when David Lloyd-George proposed the 'invented tradition' of a Welsh ceremony, complete with white-draped druids and bards, in hope of bolstering his Welsh Liberal power base against the inroads of the new Labour Party.

In private Elizabeth could see the funny side. The bulbous coronet with which she had to crown her son extinguished Charles like 'a candle snuffer', she confided to Noël Coward. But she played her part with a straight face and the mini-coronation proved another massive popular success. There has been 'a remarkable revival of interest in the British Royal

Family,' remarked the *Yorkshire Post* as the decade drew to a close – 'royalty mania', sniffed the metropolitan *Sunday Times*.

Either way, after her initial missteps, the Queen had managed to align the monarchy with the new spirit of the times. Carnaby Street trendiness contained a fond element of royal homage, from Union Jack blazers to The Beatles' *Sergeant Pepper* LP, whose sleeve design was a Victorian Jubilee pastiche. 'Buck House' might not quite be swinging with the sixties, but it had developed a refreshing and modern bounce to its step – and the credit for that went to Elizabeth's ability to identify her mistakes and to correct them. With the help of the 'goggle box' she had once considered an enemy, she had not only buried the tired

CANDLE SNUFFER.
Elizabeth II invests her son Charles as Prince of Wales, watched by the Home Secretary and future Prime Minister James Callaghan. 1ˢᵗ July 1969

rhetoric of the Second Elizabethan Age, she had given it fresh meaning.

Royal Family, of course, was a double-edged sword, as perceptive critics like Milton Shulman pointed out at the time. Showing the royals to be mere mortals could have catastrophic consequences – and the catastrophes of the next three decades were to prove that in spades. But the Queen and the monarchy were riding high for the time being, with the BBC's 40 hours or so of unshown footage locked away from sight in high-security vaults. The film cans were labelled 'Religious Programming'.

4

Daylight in upon magic
1969–1981

Prince Charles was invested Prince of Wales at Caernarfon Castle on 1st July 1969, and the moment the ceremony was over, the untried twenty-year-old stepped off the podium to embark on a week-long tour of his principality. Anti-English feeling was running high – a Welsh nationalist had been blown up by his own bomb a few days earlier. There were death threats and fears that the trip would prove a flop.

But Charles's diffident eagerness charmed all he met. Happy crowds greeted the Prince everywhere and he arrived back at Windsor anxious to share the joy of achievement with his family – to find that no one had waited up. His father and sister had gone to bed, and his mother was in London with a cold. It was Charles's first major venture in the family business, and the family took it for granted.

Charles was already a self-pitying character – 'whiney' in the robust opinion of his mother's Private Secretary, Martin Charteris. Brooding on his lonely homecoming, the Prince stored up the memory for twenty years, then poured out his resentment in his 1994 biography by Jonathan Dimbleby who, with Charles's blessing, described his mother's parenting as 'detached', and his father's rebukes – often mocking and delivered in front of a whole table of people – as 'very bullying' and 'inexplicably harsh'.

Much more to Charles's taste was the 'mission accomplished' letter that he received a few days later from his great-uncle 'Dickie' Mountbatten.

'Confidential reports on naval officers are summarised by numbers ...' wrote Mountbatten, 'pretty poor 2 or 3, very good 7 or 8 ... Your performance since you went with Fleet coverage to Wales rates you at 9 in my opinion.'

It was the beginning of a warm correspondence between two royal oddballs who suddenly discovered they were soulmates. From being a great-uncle who gave good gadget-type presents, Lord Mountbatten became the guiding light of Charles's life, the grandfather he never had – while Mountbatten found in Charles the attentive, mouldable son that Philip had refused to be. For the next ten years Mountbatten provided the overt combination of guidance, praise and constructive rebuke that Charles felt he had never received from his own mother and father – 'unable or unwilling', as the Prince explained it to Dimbleby, to give him the 'affection and appreciation' that he craved.

'You see Charles laughing and relaxing and thoroughly at ease with his parents,' says a courtier. 'And at those moments you'd think there were no problems. But, in fact, they do not have a relationship where dialogue on personal matters is possible.'

Lord Mountbatten filled the gap. Playing to Charles's sense of history, Uncle Dickie drew on the memories of his friendship with the last Prince of Wales – 'your Uncle David' – to lay down many lessons, particularly on the subjects of love, sex and the choice of a wife.

'I believe, in a case like yours,' he told Charles, 'that a man should sow his wild oats and have as many affairs as he can before settling down. But, for a wife, he should choose a suitable and sweet-charactered girl before she meets anyone else she might fall for.'

Fuck 'em all, in other words, then marry a virgin. It was the old-fashioned protocol for high-born husbands, and it would

FIRST LOVE.
*Prince Charles with Camilla Parker Bowles between polo chukkas at
Cirencester Park. July 1975*

lead to disaster, not only for Charles and the blighted marriage
he would later contract, but for the repute of his mother's
monarchy in what should have been her most glorious years.

Charles's catalyst for catastrophe was Camilla Shand, a
matter-of-fact and horsey countrywoman with a penchant
for headscarves – a younger, square-jawed version of the
Prince's own mother, and considerably less shy.

'My great-grandmother was the mistress of your great-
great-grandfather,' was her reputed come-on line when she
and Charles met. 'So how about it?'

Mrs Alice Keppel was the last of King Edward VII's many
mistresses (the novelist Henry James retitled him 'Edward the
Caresser') with a gift that her great-granddaughter inherited
for being able to laugh her royal lover out of his moods – Mrs
Keppel had made the stout, sixty-year-old monarch 'a much
pleasanter child', remarked the Duchess of Sutherland. In

Camilla's case, she had a clowning sense of fun to go with her sexual directness, sharing Charles's penchant for silly accents and *The Goon Show*, the 1950s radio comedy show from which they derived their nicknames for each other – 'Fred' and 'Gladys'.

The couple met sometime in the early 1970s, and by the summer of 1972 Camilla was a fixture at Broadlands, the Mountbattens' Hampshire estate which Uncle Dickie made available to Charles for his romantic assignations. Mountbatten took pride in making it possible for his 'honorary grandson' to enjoy there what he boasted was a 'normal healthy sex life', and Camilla certainly helped with that. She was earthy and open, appealingly lacking in either ambition or malice, and Charles freely confessed to Jonathan Dimbleby that he 'lost his heart to her almost at once.'

But Charles did not convey the strength of his feelings to Camilla at the time, for there was a Catch-22 in Uncle Dickie's formula for marital happiness. By surrendering her virtue to Charles, Camilla had surrendered her right to marry him – the bedded could not be wedded. Charles did not propose marriage to the girl to whom he had lost his heart. However much he loved her, he clearly did not consider Camilla to be princess material – and nor, evidently, did she. Within months of Charles going to sea early in 1973 on HMS *Minerva*, his first lengthy spell of naval duty, Camilla accepted the proposal of an old boyfriend, Andrew Parker Bowles, an up-and-coming young Guards officer with his own links to the Royal Family. Parker Bowles was a particularly favoured godson of the Queen Mother as well as a good friend of Charles, and had also dated Princess Anne.

So Camilla Shand became Mrs Andrew Parker Bowles on 4th July 1973, embarking on married life as a Guards officer's bride, while Prince Charles continued his quest for Uncle Dickie's 'sweet-charactered girl'. Fred and Gladys, meanwhile, were left with the memories of their intense love for each other that would not, in the end, go away.

When there is a select committee on the Queen, the
charm of royalty will be gone. Its mystery is its life.
We must not let in daylight upon magic.

Walter Bagehot, *The English Constitution, 1867*

After seventeen years on the throne, Elizabeth II was running out of money.

'We go into the red next year,' Prince Philip cheerily told NBC's *Meet the Press* during a tour of America in the autumn of 1969, explaining how inflation of 126 per cent had wreaked havoc with the arrangements made to finance the monarchy at the beginning of the reign, forcing him to sell 'a small yacht' and to consider giving up polo. 'We may have to move into smaller premises, who knows?'

'My heart bleeds,' responded Willie Hamilton, the anti-monarchist Labour MP, speaking on behalf of those who had no yachts to turn into ready cash. The British economy as a whole was faring disastrously. Once standing at a mighty $4.03 to the pound, sterling was devalued to $2.40 in 1967, and three years later unemployment reached its highest level since 1940. The humiliating figures were released on the morning of 18th June 1970, polling day, and in the day's voting that followed – the first general election in which eighteen-year-olds could vote – Harold Wilson's Labour government was swept from power.

The victors were the Conservatives under their new-look, non-charmed circle leader, Edward Heath. Lord Home's parting present to his party had been a mechanism to elect their leader by secret ballot, and the result was a Broadstairs builder's son with decidedly upmarket tastes – ocean-racing and organ music – and a strangulated way of pronouncing his vowels. 'Ted' Heath's 'eout!' (for 'out') became the delight of *Monty Python's Flying Circus*, the BBC-appointed satirists of the decade, along with his unconvincing heaving of the shoulders whenever he attempted to laugh.

Heath was Elizabeth's only unmarried prime minister, and her most difficult to that date. He was totally lacking in small talk – at dinner parties he either delivered a lecture or fell asleep – and his enthusiasm for the European Community, into which he took Britain in 1973, meant he had little sentiment for the Queen's beloved Commonwealth. One of his first actions as prime minister was to 'advise' Elizabeth – which, in practice meant compelling her – to cancel her plans to attend the upcoming Commonwealth Conference in Singapore, where he feared trouble over his decision to sell arms to the white apartheid government of South Africa.

But the new premier did his duty by the royal pay rise. Prior to the election Heath and Wilson had agreed on a bi-partisan approach to the tricky question of what Willie Hamilton had dubbed 'the most brazenly insensitive pay claim made in the last two hundred years.' Both parties wished to avoid appearing either disloyal or over-obsequious to the Palace in these tough times, so the solution was the setting up of a Select Committee on the Civil List,* Parliament's annual grant to the Crown. Heath packed the committee with a majority of loyal Conservative MPs, and at the end of 1971 the Commons duly approved a 4 per cent annual rise in the Civil List by a vote of 167 to 47.

The cheerfully disloyal Hamilton got in his digs just the same, though – Princess Margaret, he declared, was 'an expensive kept woman' who worked 'even less than her old Mum' – and his agitation prised open some intriguing financial details: royal sheds at Windsor were growing mushrooms sold on the open market to help defray costs, while fifty acres of blackcurrant bushes at

---

* The term went back to the 'Glorious Revolution' of 1688, when the parliaments of William and Mary started distinguishing between the costs of the civil government, including the monarchy, judges and the civil service (the 'Civil List'), as opposed to the lists of military/naval expenses.

BARON GRADE presents: Britain's MOST POPULAR FAMILY GROUP — THE WINDSORS — greatest TOP OF THE POPS SINCE THE OSMONDS!!

FRANKLIN

♫ "Singing in the Reign . . ." ♫

THE ROYALS GO SHOW BUSINESS.
Tabloid comment on the changing style of the House of Windsor.
The Sun, *30ᵗʰ December 1976*

Sandringham produced juice that was sold to the Ribena fruit cordial company.

The Select Committee's greatest disclosure was that while, contrary to popular assumptions, the Queen did *not* own Buckingham Palace or Windsor Castle – she was a tenant at the government's pleasure – she did control a substantial personal fortune on which she paid no tax at all. When, for example, Elizabeth received the dividends on her personal stock market investments from which tax had been deducted at source, her advisers would carefully reclaim that tax from the Inland Revenue.

The respected Labour Minister Michael Stewart, who had himself served for a short time in the royal household, politely suggested to Michael Adeane that people could hardly judge how much to pay the Queen through the Civil List if they had no idea how much they were already paying her through her royal tax exemption. Should she not come clean about her private wealth?

'I don't agree,' replied the Private Secretary. 'But even if I did, she wouldn't do it.'

The normally discreet Adeane had revealed a Palace secret, that when it came to preserving the royal fortune, Elizabeth was, in the slang of the time, the house of Windsor's own Bolshie shop steward.

'Not paying tax was one of the things her father told her to fight for,' said one of her senior advisers. 'It was a matter of family history.'

Queen Victoria had come to the throne penniless. Her father was so poor he had to drive his own carriage. But Victoria and subsequent generations had built up the Windsor fortune on the basis of thrifty handling of the Civil List – some called it stinginess – and not paying tax on what they saved. The family could never have retained Sandringham and Balmoral (personally-owned estates, as opposed to the government palaces where they lived rent free) if they had had to pay death duties.

The Queen Mother was particularly aware of this. Her own family, the Bowes Lyons, had suffered from 20th century inheritance levies like all other aristocrats, so whenever the question of royal taxes arose, the phone lines would grow hot between Clarence House and Buckingham Palace. Incensed by what she described as the 'venomous observations' coming from the House of Commons, Elizabeth's mother kept reminding her daughter 'not to give in'.

She need not have worried. The courtiers and accountants who spoke on Elizabeth's behalf defended well. The Queen's refusal to disclose the details of her private wealth was accepted by the Select Committee and by Parliament, along with her continuing exemption from tax. But from mushroom sheds to blackcurrant bushes – not to mention the royal yacht (£839,000 per year), postage stamps and phone calls (£52,000 per year), the annual cost of laying down wine (£12,000) and the royal laundry bill (up from £4,542 in 1952 to £7,267 in 1970) – it was the end of an era. Daylight had been let in upon magic.

Another era came to an end the following year with the news from Paris that the Duke of Windsor had been diagnosed with inoperable throat cancer. From the 'bronchial' problems of Edward VII and George V to the lung cancer of George VI, tobacco was claiming its fourth British monarch in succession.

Elizabeth had worked quite hard to settle the feud that had split the family for more than thirty years. She encouraged younger members of the family – her Gloucester and Kent cousins – to pay courtesy calls on the Windsors whenever they were in Paris, and in 1967 she invited both the Duke and his wife to the unveiling of a plaque in the Mall to the memory of Queen Mary. The Queen Mother had put a brave public face on being courteous to the woman she had described in her letters as 'the lowest of the low', but in private she remained implacable. When Prince Charles broached the possibility of further reconciliation, he was shocked by the strength of his grandmother's enmity.

Now was the last chance. It so happened that Elizabeth was due in Paris in May 1972 on a state visit to freshen up Franco-British relations ahead of Britain joining Europe, so arrangements were made for an historic face-to-face meeting in the Windsors' palace-in-exile in the Bois de Boulogne, all hung with banners and royal coats of arms, the flunkeys in royal livery.

The Duke had been bed-ridden for weeks, but he insisted on getting up and properly dressed to meet his Queen. Weighing less than ninety pounds and perilously weak, he sat waiting for the appointed time, spruce in a blue blazer and shirt, with a French doctor in attendance and plastic drip tubes emerging from the back of his collar to flasks concealed behind a curtain. As Elizabeth entered the room, the old man rose to his feet and inclined his head sharply forward in the reflex bow he had made to his sovereign since childhood. The doctor was horrified, fearing the drip leads would become dislodged. But the ex-king sat and talked affectionately with his niece for a quarter of an hour. As she left the room, the doctor noted there were tears in her eyes.

Nine days later the Duke was dead. His body was flown to London and the Duchess followed, to stay as Elizabeth's personal guest in Buckingham Palace. She was ill and distressed, her mind wandering. She did not feel well enough to attend the Trooping the Colour ceremony where

INSIDE THE PALACE, AT LAST.
*The Duchess of Windsor looks out at the Trooping the Colour ceremony marked by a
'Lament' for her late husband, the former King Edward VIII. 3ʳᵈ June 1972*

the pipes and drums of the Scots Guards played a poignant 'Lament' to the King who had scuttled, but she drew back the curtain from her front window on the Mall to look out on the crowds as if looking beyond them.

Two days later the Duke's funeral was held in Windsor, where Clarissa Eden, wife of the former prime minister, was struck by how gently the Queen responded to the Duchess's evident confusion. Under heavy sedation and showing signs of the dementia that would mark her final years, Wallis did nervous things with her hands and kept asking questions – 'Where do I sit?' 'Is this my seat?' 'What do I do now?'

Elizabeth had had herself placed beside Wallis, and she responded to the old lady's worries with what Lady Avon described as a 'motherly and nanny-like tenderness.' She 'kept putting her hand on the Duchess's arm or glove.'

After the service, the Duke's body was laid to rest in the royal burial place at Frogmore in Windsor Great Park, near the garden where he and Bertie had played together as children. A place was reserved beside him for his wife, and Wallis was duly buried there fourteen years later – by permission of Elizabeth II, in royal ground at last.

The 'invented tradition' of the elegant but restrained lament piped on Horse Guards Parade for the Duke of Windsor – its mourning could be taken in several ways – was the brainchild of Martin Charteris, who had just succeeded Michael Adeane as Elizabeth's principal Private Secretary, after serving in a junior capacity for more than twenty years. A romantic with his tongue in his cheek, Charteris liked to say that he had fallen in love with the Queen while she was still a princess when he came for his first interview in 1950, and that he had loved her ever since. He felt a similar affection for the entire institution of the monarchy, whose function, as he saw it, was to spread 'a carpet of happiness'

across the country – never too much ahead of the times, but in trouble if it fell too far behind.

Quizzical, amusing and creative, Charteris was the spritely major domo of Elizabeth's formal and political activities. He made being Queen fun, working in partnership with Patrick Plunket, her Deputy Master of the Household since 1954 – 'one of those bachelors of easy manners and taste,' as Kenneth Rose put it, 'who are always in demand at court.'

A friend since childhood through family links with the Bowes Lyon clan, Plunket was Elizabeth's social impresario. Never were flowers better arranged, or menus so expertly chosen. Before Christmas or birthdays, Plunket haunted Burlington Arcade and the smarter Mayfair streets, bringing back a selection of classy and original gifts from which the Queen could make her choice without going to the shops.

'Patrick was like a step-brother to her,' remembers a friend.

He arranged excursions – trips to cinemas and discreet lunches with friends in smart restaurants. He also danced with the Queen at parties while Philip was kicking up his heels with someone else. Plunket would waltz Her Majesty round and 'drop her off' with a new partner, who would not have dared to come up to her himself.

Better than anyone else – Philip included – Plunket knew how to handle Elizabeth, coaxing her gently out of her obstinacies. If an idea came from Patrick, the Queen would take direction, brightening up her cautious nature. It was Plunket who revived her love of art that had been flattened by Queen Mary's heavy-handed tours and lectures. At one late-night reception in the mid-1970s, Elizabeth led a group of guests into the palace picture gallery and gave them a guided tour that cast the allegedly 'philistine' monarch in a new light.

'She took such delight in her paintings,' remembers one of the party. 'She knew everything about them.'

That was down to Patrick. Along with the quick-witted Charteris and the Australian William Heseltine in the Press

Office, Plunket completed a royal team for the 1970s of particular lightness and style – with Porchie doing his bit at the stables. In 1974, Elizabeth's home-bred filly Highclere won the 1,000 Guineas at Newmarket, then went over to Chantilly and won the French Oaks.

These were rare consolations in a time of darkness – and, for some, despair. The early-to-mid-1970s were the most disastrous years in post-war British economic history, with rampant inflation, a prolonged stock market crash, rebellious trade unions and a doubling of energy prices following the OPEC oil embargo of 1973. Edward Heath's solution was to confront the unions – particularly the miners – and to put Britain on half time working. His 'Three Day Week' had shops operating by candlelight, office workers wearing overcoats at their desks, and a TV curfew that shut down all the television channels before 10.30 pm.[†]

The Three Day Week proved Heath's Armageddon, leading to the return of Harold Wilson and a Labour government in March 1974, first with a Commons minority, then, following a second election in October, with a working majority of three. 'Who governs Britain?' had been the Tories' election slogan, and though the answer was confused, it definitely was not Ted Heath. The Conservatives wasted little time in dumping their musical yachtsman in February 1975, turning to his former Education Secretary, Margaret Thatcher, hitherto noted for abolishing the free milk given to children in junior schools. 'Mrs Thatcher, Milk Snatcher' was Britain's first (and, to the present date, only) female major party leader, but she did not offer a cuddly prospect for the future.

---

† Heath's original ordinance instructed all three channels to cease broadcasting at 10.30, but the simultaneous shutdowns led to such a sudden call on the water supplies from baths, lavatory cisterns and taps for cups of tea, that the closedowns had to be staggered.

In the course of this largely self-inflicted domestic Suez, the Royal Family was inflicting some quite severe damage upon itself. After a few years of happiness, the 1960 marriage of Princess Margaret to the photographer Tony Armstrong Jones, ennobled as Lord Snowdon in 1961, had crumbled into a decade or more of mutual infidelity as they acted out a royal version of the fashionable idea of an 'open marriage'.

'I was rather shocked,' wrote Snowdon to his wife as he headed for another long photographic assignment abroad, 'that you took such pride in telling me that you had had only three half-hearted affairs and [that] it was much better when I was in India. All I ask is not to make it too obvious.'

The promiscuous Snowdon had affairs of his own – 'If it moves,' said one of his friends, 'he'll have it' – and he indulged in gestures of scarcely credible viciousness, compiling lists of 'Things I Hate About You' that he left in the book Margaret was reading, or lying around for her to find. 'You look like a Jewish manicurist,' read one message in a glove drawer, according to his authorised biographer, Anne De Courcy.

Wounded and less cunning, Margaret sought consolation with a string of unconventional companions: Robin Douglas-Home, the jazz pianist and author (and nephew of the former prime minister), who committed suicide shortly after their affair had ended; the gangster actor John 'Biffy' Bindon who had spent time in prison (he claimed a close relationship, Margaret denied it); and in 1973, an attractive young landscape gardener eighteen years her junior, Roddy Llewellyn.

For years Fleet Street had tried to ignore the ill-concealed secret of the Snowdons' deteriorating marriage. Many journalists knew about it through Snowdon's much praised work for the recently established *Sunday Times* 'Colour Supplement'. There was lingering guilt, perhaps, at the media pressures that had aborted Margaret's bid for happiness with Peter Townsend, and an enduring convention among the

The Queen at Aberdeen Airport with her dogs. In the foreground, lower right, a 'dorgi' – the product of a mating between a royal corgi and a dachshund of Princess Margaret. August 1974

press barons, every one of them titled, to look the other way when it came to the Royal Family's 'private' behaviour.

That changed in 1969.

'Titles?' declared Rupert Murdoch, the Australian press magnate who purchased both the *News of the World* and *The Sun* in that year. 'The only titles I want are more newspapers.'

Within months Murdoch and his editor Larry Lamb had transformed *The Sun* from a dreary Labour broadsheet into a snappy populist tabloid whose success derived from a tasty soufflé of sex, sport and scandal – its topless 'Page Three Girls' entered the language – all whisked up with a raucous dose of disrespect. Murdoch was not afraid of anybody, and the *News of the World* proved it in February 1976 when one of its journalists, masquerading as a schoolteacher, joined an upmarket group of tourists visiting the 'private' Caribbean island of Mustique and snapped a picture of Princess Margaret and the bare-chested Roddy Llewellyn relaxing at a table near the beach.

Other papers had been dropping hints at the three-year relationship between Margaret and Llewellyn, but Murdoch's front page photo socked it on the chin. Within a month, on 19th March 1976, it was announced that the Queen's sister and her husband were legally separating – leading, two years later, to the House of Windsor's first high-level divorce.

Friday 19th March 1976 was also the day when Harold Wilson announced that he was stepping down – and that was no coincidence. The Labour Prime Minister, who may already have been detecting symptoms of the Alzheimer's disease that was to mark the final years of his life, had been planning to retire around the age of sixty. So he nobly suggested to Elizabeth that he would schedule his announcement for the same moment as the Snowdons' bad news.

'He came back from the palace with some glee,' recalled Wilson's Press Secretary, Joe Haines. 'He'd made this arrangement with the Queen, he said, to blank out the separation by announcing his resignation on the same day. Having worked on popular newspapers, I was doubtful.'

Haines's doubts were justified. Wilson's resignation was announced at 11.30 in the morning, Princess Margaret's separation at 5.00 pm.

'The papers all went for the later, sexier story,' recalled the Press Secretary.

The royal scandal pushed the gallant Prime Minister straight off the front page.

1976 seemed no moment to be planning a festive jubilee (1977 would see the twenty-fifth anniversary of Elizabeth's accession), particularly after Patrick Plunket, the designated organiser of the celebration, succumbed to cancer the previous year, aged only fifty-two. Elizabeth was devastated.

'She had to watch him withering away,' remembers a friend. 'It was just tragic.'

After Plunket's death the Queen joined a fund organised by friends to raise a little gazebo at Windsor in his memory, granting permission for him to be buried in the royal cemetery at Frogmore – a Queen Victoria-style distinction she bestowed on no other servant or courtier. Among the royal working circle, Porchie now became Elizabeth's principal friend and confidant – the only person, Princess Anne once remarked, who could be sure of being put through to her mother on the phone at any time without question.

'He had the horse news,' explains a friend, 'and that was the news she really wanted to hear.'

Martin Charteris took charge of the Jubilee preparations, bouncing ideas off William Heseltine, who had moved on from the press office to become an assistant private secretary. One of their challenges was to devise the monarchy's first truly post-Victorian street spectacle, since the withdrawal from east of Suez had created a shortage of exotically-garbed imperial warriors to parade through the capital – or warriors of any kind. In place of marching bands, London was offered its first ever royal 'walkabout', an informal chat-and-sometimes-touch procedure that Heseltine had helped devise in 1970 on a royal tour to Australia and New Zealand. As the Queen emerged from her Jubilee service of thanksgiving in St Paul's cathedral on 7th June 1977, she did not board a car to her next destination – she walked half a mile through the streets to the Mansion House, shaking hands and talking to the people on one side, while her husband worked the crowd on the other.

'We've come here because we love you,' said an office girl in her early twenties.

'I can feel it, and it means so much to me,' replied Elizabeth, seeming genuinely moved.

Working with the author Philip Ziegler, Mass-Observation mounted a 1977 version of its original 1935 Jubilee study, charting the transactions of the royal walkabout (George Orwell's direct monarch-to-people connection come true), while also reporting the other flowering of the first non-military jubilee – 12,000 or more street parties that sprang up in every corner of Britain. According to the satirists of *Private Eye*, even the suburb of Neasden, with its fictitious celebrities Sid and Doris Bonkers, local football star 'Baldy' Pevsner and launderette magnate Colonel 'Buffy' Cohen, rose to the occasion with a grand symphony concert staged 'with the Board of Trade Choir'.

SILVER JUBILEE.
A street party in Belfast, Northern Ireland. July 1977

'This is great, man, just great,' enthused a [real-life] long-haired student as he surveyed the great British tradition of bazaar, raffle and jumble sale given royal shape in a Worcester cul-de-sac.

The party's organiser, an electrical shop steward, explained that the residents of the cul-de-sac included a pipe-fitter, a factory foreman, a chemist, a garage manager, a butcher and the local Anglican priest who had said a grace to open the proceedings – plus a character 'who has been on social security for 4–5 years, refused to work and is regarded as the local layabout.' This jubilee gathering provided a wonderful opportunity, said the Labour stalwart, to observe Britain's 'working class culture ... something which is fast disappearing.'

It would disappear even more rapidly in the desperate years that followed. Economically, it seemed, Britain was trapped in a spiral of decline. The 'Winter of Discontent' of 1978–79 saw James Callaghan, Harold Wilson's successor, tussling with the unions – theoretically his own supporters – as bitterly as had Edward Heath, but refusing to admit it when he returned from a sunny summit conference in Guadeloupe in January 1979.

'That's a judgement that *you* are making,' he retorted to a journalist who asked him at London Airport about 'the mounting chaos' in the country. 'I promise you that if you look at it from the outside (and perhaps you are taking rather a parochial view), I don't think that other people in the world would share the view that there is mounting chaos.'

'CRISIS? WHAT CRISIS?' was the headline in *The Sun* next morning, and four months later Callaghan lost the May 1979 general election. When the incoming Prime Minister drew up her post-election honours list, the roll call of new knights included Sir Albert 'Larry' Lamb, editor of *The Sun*.

Margaret Thatcher could be more royal than the Queen. 'We are a grandmother,' was her reaction to the news of her son Mark's first child, and when, in 1982, the time came for a march-past by the victorious British troops from the Falklands, she decided that she, not Elizabeth II, should stand on the podium.

But this was never her attitude in the royal presence.

'Margaret was a fervent royalist,' remembers her adviser, Tim Bell. 'When it came to anything to do with the Queen, she was no longer the Iron Lady, she was Margaret Roberts, the shopkeeper's daughter from Grantham. She even curtseyed to Sarah Ferguson, for Christ's sake.'

Only six months older than the Queen, Margaret Thatcher was Elizabeth's first prime minister of her own generation, and would turn out to be her longest-serving premier ever. For the entire decade of the 1980s, male chauvinist Britain was unique in the world in having a female head of state alongside a female head of government. But they were women with very different styles. A prime minister who loved a row was teamed with a monarch who would do anything she could to avoid one.

The difference became clear in their earliest interactions, a rerun in many respects of 1971, when Ted Heath had prevented Elizabeth from attending CHOGM, the Commonwealth Heads of Government Meeting in Singapore.

'She greatly regretted letting Ted stop her from going to Singapore,' recalled Martin Charteris. 'I think she was determined it was not going to happen again ... Singapore was the one Commonwealth Conference that was really sour and bad-tempered, and that was because she couldn't attend. If she's there, you see, they behave. It's like Nanny being there.'

Margaret Thatcher's contempt for the Commonwealth was one of her few points of agreement with Edward

WORKING TOGETHER.
The Queen and Mrs Thatcher as seen by Today *newspaper.*
16ᵗʰ July 1986

Heath. CHOGM, she would explain in private, stood for Compulsory Handouts to Greedy Mendicants ('Coons Holidaying On Government Money' was the offering of her husband Denis). The new Prime Minister could only foresee trouble if she attended the CHOGM scheduled to meet in August 1979 in the Zambian capital of Lusaka, since its agenda was topped by the fourteen-year-old problem of UDI‡ Rhodesia and its white settler regime with whom she sympathised. That summer Mrs Thatcher had refused to provide parliamentary time in Westminster to push through

‡ UDI was the Unilateral Declaration of Independence signed by Southern Rhodesia's white settler leader Ian Smith and his cabinet colleagues on 11th November 1965.

economic sanctions against the white rebels, to the fury of the black African leaders she would have to meet at CHOGM.

'Margaret was physically scared about Lusaka,' remembers one of her colleagues. 'There were Africans who regarded her as evil and she knew that. She did not want to go.'

The Queen had no reason for such fears. Her even-handed approach to racial matters was celebrated among her non-white Commonwealth premiers, and the success of her Silver Jubilee, coinciding with her entry into her fifties, had given her greater self-assurance.

'I've no doubt the Queen dug in her heels over Lusaka,' recalls one of the officials involved. 'Only she and Margaret Thatcher know what went on in their audiences, and it would never have been a matter of going head to head ... I imagine the Queen would have pointed out all the momentum of the Foreign Office telegrams she had been reading ... all the work that the FO had put into it, what the Commonwealth wanted and what she felt she had to do for them – that she really felt she should go.'

In her first major foreign policy decision as prime minister, Margaret Thatcher bowed to her sovereign's judgement.

'It actually gave Margaret courage,' recalled her Foreign Secretary, Lord Carington. 'Her monarch was going. It was her duty to go as well.'

As her plane taxied to a halt in the Zambian capital, Mrs Thatcher took a pair of sunglasses out of her handbag.

'She thought she might be attacked with acid thrown in her face,' recalled Carington. '"Don't worry," I told her. "They're going to love you."'

The Queen's presence brought calm to the potentially fractious proceedings.

'Everybody had a little hut,' remembered Carington. 'She had a grand hut and she held court in her hut. It was extraordinary the effect she had on everyone.'

As the Commonwealth leaders arrived one by one for their private sessions in the grand hut – actually a suburban bungalow with a chiming doorbell – the Queen talked to them about everything except Rhodesia.

'She would know who was in the clutches of the IMF,' recalled the Commonwealth Secretary, Sir Sonny Ramphal. 'Who had got what political scandal raging. She'd know the family side of things, if there were children or deaths in the family. She'd know about the economy, she'd know about elections coming up.'

Elizabeth's command of detail made each president and prime minister feel they were talking to a friend who cared particularly about them and their country – a royal master class in diplomacy.

'It was another bit of the glue,' as Sonny Ramphal put it, 'that made them a collective.'

'If Lusaka had gone wrong,' said Lord Carington, 'I think it not impossible that the Commonwealth would have broken up.'

As it was, the presiding sense of common purpose inspired by Elizabeth led to a unanimous final communiqué – even Margaret Thatcher abandoned her reservations. CHOGM Lusaka set up a process of mediation under Lord Carington's chairmanship at Lancaster House in London that, in less than three months, was able to negotiate an end to the white settler rebellion, restore international recognition to Zimbabwe/Rhodesia, and pave the way to democratic black majority rule. By the end of the process Margaret Thatcher came to feel that the Lancaster House Agreement signed on 21st December 1979 was one of her finest achievements.

The Lancaster House Agreement called for a team of British civil servants and officers to fly out to Zimbabwe to supervise the country's restoration to legality, and its Senior Military Liaison Officer was Major Andrew Parker Bowles. Charles and Camilla took full advantage of his absence.

'Ma'am,' a senior courtier informed the Queen, 'the Prince of Wales is having an affair with the wife of a brother officer, and the regiment don't like it.'

Charles had turned to Camilla in his grief following the IRA assassination of Lord Mountbatten in August 1979. 'A mixture of desperate emotions swept over me,' he wrote in his diary '– agony, disbelief, a kind of wretched numbness.'

In his final months, Mountbatten had several times felt moved to lecture Charles on his 'unkind and thoughtless' behaviour that risked 'beginning on the downward slope which wrecked your Uncle David's life and led to his disgraceful abdication.' Part of the problem was the Prince's frenetic womanising, inspired by his belated discovery of the eagerness with which many of the fair sex would surrender to the allure of royalty.

'Call me Arthur!'§ he would instruct his one-night stands, according to Luis Basualdo, his debauched polo-playing companion, who would arrange the assignation and then eavesdrop outside.

In this context, the Prince's switch from bed-hopping to the arms of Camilla could be seen as a step in a more positive direction. The couple had become ever more solid friends as Camilla raised her family, confiding in each other and particularly enjoying the game of dissecting and passing judgement on the succession of women who moved through his life. It gave Camilla a special closeness to her lover – and also a faintly sinister power.

People did not like what they saw when Charles flew out to Zimbabwe in April 1980 to represent his mother at the independence ceremony, for he took Camilla along, ostensibly to be reunited with her husband. On the journey out the couple remained shut away together, giggling in the private quarters of the plane. At a formal dinner in Harare

---

§ The Prince was christened Charles Philip Arthur George.

BANNED.

The BBC refused to broadcast the Sex Pistols' punk rock critique of the National Anthem during the Silver Jubilee of 1977, but later admitted that the song had reached number one in that year

their ostentatious flirting extended to Charles fumbling below the table with his mistress while her husband stoically looked the other way. The incident was so flagrant that reports of it reached the Queen.

'There are times,' said a courtier, 'when the Queen and Prince Philip are just plain baffled by this eldest son they have produced.'

Elizabeth and her husband could only hope for one way out of the mess. Charles was now over thirty. He needed to locate Uncle Dickie's sweet-charactered young girl and settle down with her as soon as possible. Perhaps she could solve the problem.

5

Whatever 'in love' means
1981–1995

To get along well with Queen Elizabeth II was 'no big deal', Diana Spencer used to remark to her friends. She had known the Queen from childhood – in fact, she had grown up in Her Majesty's Norfolk back garden. Diana's father Johnny Spencer, who became the 8th Earl Spencer in 1975, was the tenant of Park House, a ten-bedroom farmhouse with cattle-farming acreage on the Sandringham estate. So the young Spencers – Diana (born 1961), her elder sisters Sarah and Jane and her younger brother Charles – got to know the 'big house' quite well when they would cycle up to play with Elizabeth's 'second' family. Diana came between Andrew and Edward in age and used to watch movies with them on the comfy sofas of the Sandringham 'cinema'. *Chitty Chitty Bang Bang* was a Christmas regular.

The links grew closer when Diana's middle sister Jane married Robert Fellowes, the quiet young Assistant Private Secretary who started working at the palace in 1977.

'Robert is the only one of my private secretaries I have held in my arms,' Elizabeth remarked on one occasion, referring to the days when she had cradled the newly-arrived baby son of Billy Fellowes, the estate manager at Sandringham – as, indeed, she had cradled the baby Spencers.

There was every reason for the Queen to welcome Diana in September 1980 when Charles invited his latest marriage prospect up to Scotland. Johnny and his first wife Frances had divorced since the happy days at Park House, and some said that Diana had been adversely affected by the bitter custody battle that followed. But the nineteen-year-old seemed anything but troubled. She was cheerful and easy-going, adapting to the Balmoral routine – just the sort of house guest that Her Majesty appreciated.

'We went stalking together,' remembered fellow guest Patti Palmer-Tomkinson, a friend of Prince Charles. 'We got hot, we got tired, she fell into a bog, she got covered in mud, laughed her head off, got puce in the face, her hair glued to her forehead because it was pouring with rain … She was a sort of wonderful English schoolgirl who was game for anything.'

The whole family liked her. Edward and Andrew competed with their elder brother to sit beside Diana at evening picnics, and Prince Philip clearly appreciated her good looks. Charles had finally picked himself a winner.

The British press felt just the same. Lurking outside in the woods and on the right-of-way footpaths of Balmoral that autumn was the new breed of royal correspondent that had evolved in the late 1970s as Charles's quest for a wife had become a media obsession. Binoculars, long lenses, running shoes and aluminium stepladders for peering over inconvenient walls and hedges made up their standard equipment, together with a recently developed, brick-sized device with an aerial – 'the mobile'. The sleuths had already caught glimpses of Charles's latest companion as she sat on the riverbank watching him fish, and it was a Murdoch paper that tapped its police contacts for her name then splashed it on the front page.

'He's In Love Again,' proclaimed *The Sun* on the morning of 8th September 1980. 'Is this the real thing for Charles at last?'

SHY DI.
Lady Diana Spencer with her charges at the Young England Kindergarten, Pimlico. September 1980

In this very first story *The Sun* coined the famous nickname 'Lady Di' to which, a few days later, it added 'Shy Di', when Diana returned to London to find photographers surrounding her flat in Coleherne Court, a red brick mansion block near Earls Court. Every morning she had to make her way demurely through a scrum of scuffling cameras, notepads and microphones, keeping her head down and allowing herself just the occasional giggle.

Diana was working as a part-time nanny and nursery teacher at the Young England Kindergarten in Pimlico, and ten days later a photographer persuaded the head teacher to let him take just one quick snap of her suddenly famous assistant, after which he promised to go away and stop frightening the children. Diana duly scooped up a child and stepped outside – just as the sun came out from behind a cloud and backlit her cotton skirt.

'I knew your legs were good,' commented Prince Charles when he saw the picture that was syndicated around the world, 'but I didn't realise they were *that* spectacular.' The Prince also appreciated, according to an indiscreet friend, Diana's 'fabulous bazookahs'.

Looking back, the Young England Kindergarten photograph can be seen as the beginning of Diana's literally fatal addiction to getting her picture in the papers. But at the time it seemed no more than an innocent mistake, and Elizabeth was supportive. The girl was going through the 1980s' version of the 'Where's Philip?' harassment that she had suffered before her own engagement was announced.

'In those early days,' remembered one of Elizabeth's friends, 'she looked out at Diana coping all on her own and she really felt for her.'

In November 1980 the Queen made a rare intervention in response to newspaper provocation, instructing her Press Secretary Michael Shea to deny a *Sunday Mirror* story that claimed Diana had spent two nights with Prince Charles in the royal train while it stood in a Wiltshire siding. Those in the know asserted that the mystery blonde seen boarding the train was, in fact, Camilla. But at that stage Elizabeth did not care. Her concern was to protect the reputation of a young woman that she was now viewing as a future member of the family.

'Go away! Can't you leave us alone?' she shouted from her car in a rare display of temper that Christmas, when the 'rat pack' descended on Sandringham. The hordes of reporters and photographers crowding around the house day and night created a siege atmosphere. Diana duly arrived, but cut short her visit – the girl, still only nineteen, was in an impossible situation.

Characteristically, Elizabeth said nothing to Charles directly, but she did speak to Philip, and in his role as head of the family her husband sat down to write their eldest son a carefully considered letter that he sent to Charles in the early weeks of 1981.

Media pressure was creating an intolerable situation, wrote Philip, which meant that Charles must come to a rapid decision. Either he must offer Diana his hand in marriage, which would clearly please the country – and would also, his father made clear, please the rest of the family – or he must break off the relationship to avoid Diana's reputation being 'compromised'.

'Read it!' Charles would exclaim in later years, whipping the letter out of his breast pocket in fury.

'At some stage when the marriage started going wrong,' recalled one of those to whom he had shown the note, 'he dug this letter out, folded it up and started carrying it round and showing it to everyone ... It was his attempt to say that he was forced into it.'

'It was actually very constructive and trying to be helpful,' said someone who had read the note under Charles's indignant gaze. 'It certainly ... [did] not read as an ultimatum.'

Barbara Cartland, the romantic novelist and mother of Johnny Spencer's second wife Raine, shrewdly remarked in 1981 that newspaper pressure and publicity was creating 'the first time the Queen of England has been chosen by referendum.' But Prince Philip's 'ultimatum' letter written on behalf of himself and his wife could be seen as having created the very opposite – an old-fashioned marriage of compulsion.

Prince Charles certainly saw it that way.

'Can you find the words to sum up how you feel today?' the couple were asked when their engagement was made public on 24th February 1981, '… in love?'

'Whatever "in love" means,' came Charles's famous reply. 'Put your own interpretation on it.'

The summer of 1981 was marked by the most bitter and destructive race riots that Britain had even seen. In the ghettos of Handsworth (Birmingham), Chapeltown (Leeds), Toxteth (Liverpool), Brixton (South London) and Moss Side (Manchester) angry crowds of black youths protested at the new stop and search powers of the police, the so-called 'Sus' laws introduced by Margaret Thatcher's Conservative government. Unemployment continued to rise – to 2.5 million, a level not seen since the 1930s – and the Iron

RIOT GEAR.
Police get ready for action in Toxteth, Liverpool. July 1981

Lady's refusal to modify her cost-cutting, monetarist policies created an atmosphere of confrontation. News bulletins presented a bizarre combination of inner cities in flames alongside wedding dress speculation.

They also presented the reassuring picture of the Queen steadying her horse to ride resolutely onwards when an unemployed youth fired off six blank cartridges at her on the Mall as she rode to the Trooping the Colour ceremony on 13th June.

'If there had been real bullets in that gun, he would have shot the Queen,' said the St John's Ambulance man who wrestled the assailant to the ground.

The sang-froid of Elizabeth, 'ashen-faced' according to the *News of the World* but 'cool as a cucumber', was the stoic model people chose to follow that confusing summer. There was a marriage to celebrate, and the romantic dreams embodied in wedding fantasies proved powerfully more attractive than worrying too much about the world as it really was.

'Go on, give her a kiss!' urged Prince Andrew as his elder brother went out on the balcony for yet another appearance with Diana on the afternoon of 29th July 1981. No one had ever kissed on the palace balcony before, and Charles knew he must get his mother's permission for the extra gesture – which she gave with a smile. Her Majesty was as giddy as everyone else with the high emotion of the day.

That evening she watched it all on large screen televisions set up in Claridge's. Dry martini in hand, the Queen watched herself intently, pointing delightedly whenever the cameras caught one of her famous glum faces. It was noticed that she beamed with particular pleasure when images of her new daughter-in-law appeared.

Prince Philip danced a lot with Princess Grace of Monaco. He was wearing a jaunty straw hat which said 'Charles and Diana' in red, white and blue around the hat band, and it was only with great difficulty that Elizabeth

'GIVE HER A KISS!'
Charles and Diana, following their wedding in St Paul's Cathedral on the balcony of Buckingham Palace. 29ᵗʰ July 1981

prevailed upon her husband to take it off before they walked out into the street. By then it was 1.30 in the morning, and the Queen hitched up her skirt and did a little jig as she said her goodbyes.

'I'd love to stay and dance all night,' she said.

Three weeks later she welcomed the couple back from their ocean-going honeymoon with similar gusto. Two hundred staff and estate workers lined the drive leading to the front door of Balmoral as the honeymooners were pulled up from the castle gates in an old pony trap drawn by four muscular Highland retainers. The Queen ran alongside, hopping and skipping to keep up, while her husband pedalled on an ancient bicycle, Paul Newman-Butch Cassidy style, before shooting off ahead to be waiting at the front door.

That was euphoric August. By the end of September 1981 the atmosphere at Balmoral was very different. Charles and Diana had arrived in Scotland to find the grouse season in full swing, with its own rituals and timetable. Every morning after breakfast the men would head off to the moors, leaving the women to join them later for lunch. The Queen would deal with her boxes and letters till midday or 12.15, when she would appear in the hall in her headscarf, tweeds and sensible shoes, ready to lead the party to the Land Rovers waiting outside. It went without saying that no one should be a minute late.

'So there we'd all be waiting in the hall,' recalled a guest, 'making polite conversation – and no Diana. So after a time the Queen would send off a footman, and he'd come back looking embarrassed. "Sorry, Ma'am, the Princess of Wales will not be joining the party for lunch."'

Elizabeth would go very silent. Friends saw the danger signs – the pursed lips, the extra quick blink of the eyes. Staying in your room at lunchtime was something you only did if you were ill or rather odd. Then the smile would return, a trifle strained, and Her Majesty would move off resolutely in picnic mode.

'The Queen's thought in those days,' said a friend, 'was that Diana was a "new girl" who was finding it very difficult to get used to things.'

It was rather more complicated than that, for the bitter break-up of her parents' marriage had actually affected Diana quite profoundly. Her sister Sarah reacted to stress by starving herself – the long-recognised syndrome of *anorexia nervosa*. Diana's reaction was to stuff herself with food, then stick her fingers down her throat to induce herself to vomit – the condition of *bulimia nervosa*, that had only been given a medical name two years earlier.

Fragile though she was, Diana had not suffered from bulimia when she impressed everyone with her jolliness at Balmoral the previous September. Now she did, however, and the principal reason why her stability had been thrown so drastically out of kilter was the astonishing discovery she had made in the intervening year – that her new husband's loyalty and deepest emotions were committed to another woman.

To start with, Diana had been charmed by the almost motherly concern that Camilla, fourteen years her senior, appeared to be showing for her welfare: inviting her to stay at Bolehyde, the Parker Bowles's home near Charles's country mansion at Highgrove, taking her to the races and confiding in her, as a former girlfriend, about the little ways to please and get round the often difficult Prince – 'Don't push him into doing this, don't do that.' But Diana began to notice how Camilla always seemed to be on the inside track.

'She knew so much about what he was doing privately and about what we were doing privately,' she later told Andrew Morton, '… if we were going to stay at Broadlands. I couldn't understand it.'

When Diana moved into Clarence House on 24th February 1981, she found a letter on her bed from Camilla, dated two days previously, congratulating her on the just-announced engagement and suggesting lunch.

'So we had lunch. Very tricky indeed. She said: "You are not going to hunt are you?" I said: "On what?" She said: "Horse. You are not going to hunt when you go and live at Highgrove are you?" I said: "No." She said: "I just wanted to know."'

SECOND PLACE.
Camilla Parker Bowles escorts Lady Diana Spencer to watch Prince Charles ride at
Ludlow Races. January 1981

Puzzled at the time, Diana later realised Camilla was working out how she could go on meeting Charles after the marriage – and her suspicions were confirmed when, as she later told Morton, 'I ... heard him on the telephone in his bath on his hand-held saying: "Whatever happens, I will always love you." I told him afterwards that I had listened at the door and we had a filthy row.'

The openness of Charles's allegiance to his mistress was quite extraordinary. A few days before the wedding, Diana discovered in Charles's office a gold chain bracelet with a blue enamel disc bearing the intertwined initials 'G' and 'F' – Gladys and Fred. And on the honeymoon, getting ready for a white tie dinner on the royal yacht with President Sadat of Egypt, she spotted new cufflinks on Charles's wrists – two 'C's entwined like the double 'C' emblem of the fashion firm Chanel.

'Got it in one; knew exactly. "Camilla gave you those didn't she?" He said: "Yes, so what's wrong? They're a present from a friend." And, boy, did we have a row. Jealousy, total jealousy.'

Charles would later claim through Jonathan Dimbleby that the notorious 'GF' bracelet was his way of saying goodbye to Camilla, his 'Girl Friday', for 'what both of them intended to be the last time.' But what sort of husband flaunts a love token from his mistress on his honeymoon, then says to his wife 'So what's wrong?'

Diana arrived at Balmoral feeling confused and desperate, smiling one moment then breaking helplessly into tears the next. The royal way of life that had seemed to offer so many hopes and possibilities, twelve months earlier, now embodied a painful life sentence of betrayal.

'At night I dreamt of Camilla the whole time.'

Diana would later blame the unfeeling House of Windsor for not offering her more support in her impossible dilemma but, in fact, her new mother-in-law tried to help her from the start. Pondering on why the married and now royal Diana was displaying such a very different psychology from the jolly girl who had been 'game for anything' one year earlier, Elizabeth referred the problem to experts. By the end of September 1981, Diana was on a plane down to London to meet with Harley Street's best.

'All the analysts and psychiatrists you could ever dream of,' remembered the Princess, 'came plodding in trying to sort me out.'

And having done what she could to help Diana with her private demons, the Queen turned to the devils who were afflicting her public existence. Early in December the editors of Fleet Street were invited to Buckingham Palace to discuss what might be done to ease the pressure on the monarchy's delicate new recruit.

'She's not like the rest of us,' explained the Queen who joined the gathering for drinks. 'She's very young.'

'But it's difficult drawing a line between public and private,' argued Barry Askew, editor of the *News of the World*, referring to a recent incident when a photographer had pursued Diana into a village shop. 'I mean, when she's out at the shops she's in public. Why shouldn't she be photographed?'

'All she wants to do,' replied the Queen, 'is buy some wine gums without being disturbed.'

'If she wants to buy wine gums,' argued the editor, 'she should send a servant to get them.'

'That,' responded the Queen icily, 'is an extremely pompous remark, if I may say so.'

By now Diana was pregnant, and the birth of Prince William on 21st June 1982 brought a certain calm to the family turmoil. The Princess had fulfilled her primary function in rapid time – the provision of a healthy son and heir – and she had also brought into her own life a male that she could trust. Next day the Queen came to congratulate her daughter-in-law and inspect the new arrival.

'Thank goodness,' she said, woman to woman, 'he hasn't got ears like his father.'

Early on the morning of 9th July 1982, Elizabeth II was woken in Buckingham Palace by the sound of her bedroom door opening, followed by heavy, unfamiliar footsteps that appeared to be making for her bed.

'It's too early yet for tea,' she said sharply, knowing it could not be her footman, who was out exercising the corgis at that hour.

The intruder Michael Fagan, a thirty-one-year-old unemployed labourer, paid no heed. He kept walking across the room, drew back the curtains then sat down on Her Majesty's bed.

'I want to know who I am,' he later explained to the police. 'She can tell me ... I am in love with Elizabeth Regina.'

Confronted by this tousled and scruffy schizophrenic, carrying the intimidating shard of a heavy glass ashtray with which, he later said, he planned to slash his wrists, Elizabeth displayed the cool presence of mind she had shown on horseback in the Mall the previous year.

'I got out of bed,' she later related, 'put on my dressing gown and slippers, drew myself up to my full regal height [5ft 4in], pointed to the door and said "Get out!" – and he didn't.'

In his own account of the conversation, Fagan told the Queen he thought that her palace security was 'diabolical' – and so he had proved. This was his second dawn jaunt in recent nights around the royal premises, which he had entered by shinning up a drainpipe. On his last visit a few days earlier he had opened and helped himself to a swig from a bottle of wine sent to Diana and Charles to celebrate Prince William's birth.

'I have never heard the Queen so angry,' said a footman when, after two calls to the palace switchboard, a policeman eventually arrived to escort Fagan away. It was a blessing, remarked Elizabeth, that Philip had been in his own quarters at the time getting ready for a 6.00 am departure – 'I knew that all hell would break loose.'

Opinion was divided on the meaning of the tragic-comic episode, from which Fagan got away scot-free – a jury found him not guilty of the only crime with which he was charged, the 'stealing' of the wine he had sampled from Prince William's arrival gifts. There was alarm at such crass security at a moment when the IRA was more active in London than ever – ten days later two fatal explosions blew up soldiers in the capital. But the general reaction was disbelief. Like so many of the Royal Family's misadventures in the 1980s and 90s, you could not make it up if you tried.

The summer of 1982 found Britain embroiled in a good old-fashioned war. Margaret Thatcher's military expedition to the south Atlantic to recapture the Falkland Islands from Argentina was a gunboat adventure that, unlike Suez, went spectacularly well. Elizabeth was involved in four ways: as Sovereign of Great Britain, as Head of the Commonwealth which contained such enduring and inconvenient fragments of empire as the Falklands, as Head of the Armed Forces and as the mother of a combatant.

'Prince Andrew is a serving officer,' said a Palace spokesman on 1st April 1982 in response to suggestions that the Queen might like her second son exempted from military service, 'and there is no question in her mind that he should go.'

Two hundred and fifty-five Britons and 652 Argentinians died in the conflict, and Andrew risked his own life. As a helicopter pilot, he was assigned the duty of dangling huge sheets of foil as a decoy to the enemy's deadly Exocet missiles. The handsome warrior Prince returned with a long-stemmed rose clenched between his teeth, to be greeted on the quayside by his mother, and then promptly threw himself into a succession of red-blooded flings appropriate to a conquering hero.

CONQUERING HERO.
Prince Andrew is greeted by his mother at Portsmouth on his return from active service in the Falklands War. 17ᵗʰ September 1982

The tabloids found a new hero in 'Randy Andy', and when his heart settled on Sarah Ferguson, the daughter of Prince Charles's polo manager and an old acquaintance of the Queen, it was counted no obstacle that she had a 'colourful past'. She had been living in Switzerland with an ex-racing driver, Paddy McNally, who was twenty-two years older than her and a business associate of Bernie Ecclestone, the rising Grand Prix tycoon.

'Fergie' was a character, like her name, made in tabloid heaven, and her marriage to Andrew in July 1986 was a downmarket version of his elder brother's fairy tale wedding five years earlier. On the night before, the couple spiced up their version of the now hallowed pre-wedding TV interview with their own attempt at an illustrated song, which had become known in the 80s as a 'music video' – a mawkish sequence of dancing and embracing to the hit of the moment, Jennifer Rush's 'The Power of Love'.

When the couple appeared on the palace balcony the next day, they even parodied 'the kiss' that Andrew had choreographed five years earlier. As *The Times* described it:

> The Duke broadly cupped his ear to the chanting of 'Give her a kiss then!' So he gave her a kiss, not a moth's kiss, but a smacking naval kiss like a tyre explosion, or as if he were trying to clear the drains.

The slapstick collusion between audience and performers marked yet another erosion of royal distance. With mock videos and bawdy kisses, the new royal generation was taking the monarchy into the marketplace. Prince Charles published his own children's bedtime story, *The Old Man of Lochnagar*, to be outdone by Fergie, who churned out a long series of children's books on 'Budgie', a talking helicopter. Her husband packaged his photographs into a coffee table book, while his elder sister managed to fill an entire volume with *Princess Anne and Mark Phillips Talking About Horses*. It seemed that scarcely a publishing season went by without some royal author entering the fray.

The young royals' busy trading on their status made clear they could be just as vain and banal as any other attention-seeking celebrity – and if one moment crystallised that perception, it came in the summer of 1987 with the broadcasting of *It's a Royal Knockout*, a special edition of a game show in which teams of celebrities and members of the public made fools of themselves. The project marked the public debut of Elizabeth's youngest and most indulged son, Prince Edward, whose highest profile action to that point had been his ignominious departure from the Royal Marines earlier that year, after serving fewer than four months of his promised five years.

'It was a matter of the boy's self-esteem,' recalls a courtier of the time. 'We were all solidly against the *Knockout* project. But Edward had privately plotted it so far, the Queen felt she could not say no. After the Marines, it would have involved him in a second loss of face.'

SPITTING IMAGE.
Phil, Liz and friends, stars of the satirical 1984–1996 TV puppet show created by Peter Fluck and Roger Law of The Sunday Times Magazine

In the event, the sight of Edward, Fergie, Andrew and Princess Anne cheering on their teams dressed up as vegetables and throwing fake hams raised over £1 million for charity, and the event might have been written off as a cringe-making damp squib, if it had not been for the conduct of Edward at the press conference afterwards. As fifty embarrassed journalists struggled to think of something polite to ask, the twenty-three-year-old Prince began by aggressively jutting out his jaw and putting a question to them.

'Well, what do you think of it, then?'

In the painful silence that followed, Edward stormed petulantly out of the tent. An occasion designed to demonstrate how amusing young royal folk could be had ended up suggesting that one of them, at least, took himself far too seriously.

'It simply got out of control,' recalled a courtier who had been involved in the ground-breaking *Royal Family* project. 'There was a time in the mid-1980s when it seemed that every younger member of the family was their own press officer. It just went to their heads.'

What this courtier, and every senior official in Buckingham Palace, kept hoping was that the Queen would intervene and exercise the authority over her children that nobody else could. But she did nothing.

'The Queen,' said one of her close advisers, weighing his words judiciously, 'finds the boxes rather easier to organise than the children.'

The firm smack of royal authority was also lacking when *The Sunday Times*, purchased in 1981 by Rupert Murdoch and edited by Andrew Neil, a combative Scot, published an extraordinary front page story on 20th July 1986 claiming that Elizabeth II abhorred Thatcherism. Under the headline 'Queen dismay at uncaring Thatcher', sources 'close to the Queen' revealed that Her Majesty differed from her prime minister on issues ranging from Commonwealth sanctions against apartheid South Africa to the attack on Britain's traditional welfare state. Elizabeth, apparently, found the whole range of Mrs Thatcher's policies to be 'uncaring, confrontational and socially divisive.'

The article was absolutely correct. While admiring the fortitude that Mrs Thatcher had displayed in regaining the Falklands and defying the IRA attempts to murder her, notably in the Brighton bombing of October 1984, the Queen was not at ease with her prime minister's attack dog style – all the fiercer since the Conservatives' 165-seat demolition of Labour and the new Liberal-SDP Alliance in the 1983 post-Falklands election. Elizabeth was particularly dismayed by the contempt of the Thatcherite 'New Right' for the state-dominated consensus that was established by Clement Attlee in the years after World War II and had been broadly followed ever since by governments of both parties.

'Do you think Mrs Thatcher is a religious person?' she pointedly asked Robert Runcie, her Archbishop of Canterbury, in 1985.

In Thatcherite terms Her Majesty was a 'wet' – a 'super-wet', indeed. Elizabeth supported the campaigns of her black African Commonwealth leaders to end white South African apartheid, while deploring the lip-smacking ruthlessness of the New Right's assault on Britain's underclass.

'The people of Govan have got nothing,' she remarked over dinner with the Labour Party leader Neil Kinnock in 1988, discussing the derelict Glasgow ship-building district. 'I know, because I have sailed *Britannia* there.'

So far as apartheid was concerned, Elizabeth was on the right side of history. But she made the wrong prediction – in immediate material terms, at least – when it came to the Thatcherite programme of privatisation, business deregulation and the reduction of state power that, with the help of North Sea oil, provided the underpinning to twenty years of prosperity for just about everybody in Britain: by far the longest boom in her reign.

Either way, it was not for Buckingham Palace to reveal the Queen's personal opinions on any subject to anyone, let alone to a commercial newspaper. Elizabeth should instantly have sacked and disowned the source of the leak, her Press

LOW CURTSEY.
Margaret and Denis Thatcher (left) welcome their sovereign to 10 Downing Street.
4th December 1985

Secretary Michael Shea, who it soon emerged had talked too freely to Simon Freeman, a young *Sunday Times* reporter, who had given the impression he wanted background material for a long-term profile of the Queen then revealed it would all be in the paper on Sunday.

A totally-focused press spokesman would not have been fooled by such a routine newspaper trick – Shea supplemented his day job with writing novels – but Elizabeth liked her Press Secretary, as he adored her. He loved surprising reporters with positive titbits about the humour and humanity of his employer – that had been his downfall with Freeman – and Elizabeth could not bring herself to make a scene.

'Confrontation,' sighed one of the extended family regretfully, 'is just *not* her strong point.'

So Shea was allowed to limp on in the job for a few more months, having made a private apology to the Prime Minister. Ironically, it was the theoretically abrasive Thatcher who came out of the affair with more dignity.

'She went out of her way not to appear to be irritated,' one of her cabinet colleagues told the biographer Ben Pimlott – which was not only courteous but clever. The Prime Minister was planning to run for re-election in less than a year and, as another of her aides put it, 'the idea that the Queen was pissed off with Mrs Thatcher was the last bloody thing we needed.'

In April 1987 the Princess of Wales went to London's Middlesex Hospital to open the UK's first ward for the treatment of HIV/AIDS, the mysterious and deadly 'Gay Plague' first identified in 1981 and originally known as GRID, or 'Gay-Related Immune Deficiency'. Such was the stigma attached to the disease that only one of the twelve men selected to meet Diana agreed to be photographed – with his back to the camera.

But Diana shook hands with that man, and with all the other eleven patients, without wearing gloves, in a brave and brilliant gesture that went around the world.

'At that moment when she touched him,' remembered Richard Kay, a young *Daily Mail* journalist who would later become a confidant of Diana's, 'there was this extraordinary feeling of some barrier being broken. None of us could quite believe what we were seeing. The news desk kept asking, "Are you sure she wasn't wearing gloves?" She lifted the stigma – and it was also the start of her own great adventure and transformation from being a clothes horse to a woman with this inspirational mission to save.'

Diana's style of compassionate outreach would provide a dramatic counterweight to the Scrooge-like aspects of the Thatcher era – and was also seen by some as a deliberate upstaging of the chilly House of Windsor. If so, they only had themselves to blame. Middlesex Hospital had asked Buckingham Palace for a member of the Royal Family to open the ward, expressing a preference for Prince Charles, but the Palace, possibly nervous at the seedy connotations of the new disease, chose to send Diana.

By now the fractured nature of the Wales's marriage was clear to their family, staff and servants – the birth of Prince Harry in September 1984 was the surprisingly early date identified by several friends as the moment when the couple stopped 'making the effort'.

'I think Prince Charles really did try quite hard,' remembered a former private secretary. 'But there was a sense in which he always remained a bachelor, and there is a basic selfishness about bachelors.'

By 1987, the pattern was set. On Sunday evenings Diana would leave Highgrove with the boys, heading for London. The Highgrove staff would hear the water running upstairs and Charles would appear shortly afterwards in blazer and cravat, pink and groomed and smelling of spicy shampoo. With his detective, he would get in his car and make the twenty-minute drive to Middlewick House, the home to which the Parker Bowleses had recently downsized and from which Andrew Parker Bowles had that evening departed to take up his military duties for the week.

Diana herself, meanwhile, had gone on her own search for love and warmth outside her marriage, enjoying a series of romantic knockabouts that included her cheery cockney detective, Barry Mannakee (swiftly moved on to other duties), a dashing Guards officer-turned-personal riding instructor, Major James Hewitt, and a young car salesman, James Gilbey, of the Gilbey gin family, who affectionately nicknamed her 'Squidge' or 'Squidgy'.

Sensing the trouble that was brewing, a young tabloid journalist, Andrew Morton, made it his business to get on good terms with James Colthurst, a recently qualified doctor who had had a decorous flirtation with Diana in pre-Charles days and had become something of a counsellor to her. Diana wanted to get her story to the world, Colthurst told Morton after one of their games of squash together, and he had a mechanism to propose. Morton should send Diana his questions, to which she would tape-record her replies with Colthurst acting as the go-between. The doctor gave Diana deniability. When questioned about Morton, she would be able to say, 'I never met the man'.

That became the Princess's alibi when Morton's book, *Diana: Her True Story*, was serialised on 7th June 1992 in *The Sunday Times*, shocking not just Britain but the whole world with painful and intimate descriptions of Diana throwing herself down the staircase at Sandringham while pregnant with William, her attempts at self-mutilation with a penknife and, the real object of the exercise, the details of Charles's long-term infidelity with Camilla.

'I had nothing to do with it,' she assured her brother-in-law Robert Fellowes, by then Elizabeth's principal Private Secretary.

Nobody believed her.

'I could hear my wife talking,' said Prince Charles, 'as I read those words in the paper.'

The middle of June saw Royal Ascot Week, the race meeting that brought the entire clan together for the traditional week-long house party at Windsor Castle.

'The atmosphere was dreadful,' remembered one of the guests. 'Absolutely no one in the family was speaking to Diana. They were blanking her completely. She curled up in the back of the royal box in floods of tears.'

Without any real knowledge yet of how Morton had got his story, the Queen had no doubt that she and the family were victims of the most monstrous betrayal. But she and Philip held back from accusing Diana.

'If anything, they tried not to side with Charles against Diana,' said a friend. 'They were very conscious that, in a sense, she did not have a family, and that they had to try to supply her with that.'

Elizabeth fell back on the therapy that her husband called her 'dog mechanism'. She would take her corgis out for extra-long walks, bring them home, wash them, and then take them out again. In her theoretically all-powerful position the Queen found that she was actually powerless and, not for the first time, she played the constitutional monarch inside her own home, leaving her husband, as chief executive, to express their joint feelings.

During the course of the next few weeks, Prince Philip sat down at his word processor to tap out no less than four longish letters to Diana, trying to mend the painfully widening breach. He liked to do this sort of work after tea. Drawing on his past experience as a young outsider, who had had dust-ups of his own with the stuffiness of the Palace, Philip encouraged his daughter-in-law to take the longer view and assured her of his fundamental support – and of the Queen's.

'They were absolutely splendid letters,' said someone who read them, 'and in every reply she thanked him in a big way. She said in one response that she was really "touched" by all the trouble he was taking.'

'But why do you *write* all those letters?' asked two of Philip's very oldest friends. 'Wouldn't it be much better if you actually talked to her?'

'It just makes her upset,' explained the Duke, and he recounted an extraordinary story. Before the Morton book was published, he and the Queen had tried talking to Diana, he said, and to Charles as well. They had met for a 'summit meeting', an informal attempt at self-help family therapy, at which Elizabeth and her husband, as the older couple, tried to explain how they understood the problems that marriages go through and how they were both just desperate to help.

'Can you tell us what's the matter, Diana?' asked Philip, at which his daughter-in-law collapsed in tears. The Princess stayed sobbing on her own, refusing all comfort.

'Well, Charles,' enquired the Queen rather desperately, turning to her son who was fuming across the room. 'Can *you* explain to us?'

'What?' responded the Prince. 'And read it all in the newspapers tomorrow? No thank you.'

And that was the end of the first and last Royal Family therapy session.

1992 marked the fortieth anniversary of Elizabeth's accession, but there was little to celebrate. In January, embarrassing photographs of the Duchess of York's liaison with Steve Wyatt, an American playboy, were published, leading to the separation of the Yorks in March. In April, the already separated Princess Anne and Mark Phillips were divorced, and Fergie was back on the front pages in August, photographed topless beside a pool in the south of France with John Bryan, the latest American in her life and allegedly her 'financial adviser', leaning over her and ardently sucking her toes.

This scoop by the *Daily Mirror* prompted *The Sun* to publish the text of a tape it had held for some time, an intercept of Diana on New Year's Eve 1989 talking to James Gilbey, the lover who called her 'Squidgy'.*

---

* In 1992–3 most people accepted the explanation that this and the parallel recording of Charles and Camilla were accidental interceptions of wireless transmissions by random radio hams. But, in chapter 15 of her book, *The Diana Chronicles*, Tina Brown presents impressive technical evidence to suggest that the original recordings of the conversations could only have been obtained by illegal telephone bugging, which was deliberately re-broadcast in order to be 'accidentally' discovered.

"I PREFERRED IT WHEN SHE JUST USED TO SHAKE HANDS!"

Sun, 20th August, 1992

TOE-SUCKING RULES OK!
Fergie goes out in style. The Sun, *20th August 1992*

'I was very bad at lunch and I nearly started blubbing,' said Diana, describing Sandringham where she was staying. 'I just felt really sad and empty and thought "Bloody hell, after all I've done for this fucking family."'

The 'Squidgy Tapes' were nothing, however, compared to the bizarre conversation recorded that summer by a *Daily Mirror* reader in Chester and published by the paper some months later.

'Your great achievement is to love me,' declared Prince Charles to Camilla, before going on to reveal his ultimate fantasy, drawing on his interest in Buddhism and reincarnation, that he might come back in his next life as 'God forbid, a Tampax', thus realising his dream to 'just live inside your trousers.'

The burning of Windsor Castle on 20th November 1992 put the cap on it all. A curtain brushing a spotlight kindled flames that leapt into the high roof void, ravaging the north-east corner of the building. Prince Andrew organised a naval-

ANNUS HORRIBILIS.
Queen Elizabeth II examines the fire damage to Windsor Castle. 21ˢᵗ November 1992

style rescue chain to salvage all but one important picture, but nine state apartments and a hundred other rooms were destroyed or severely damaged. Television cameras caught the small, sad figure of the Queen in rain hood, mackintosh and wellington boots as she trudged around the ruins of her childhood home.

'She is devastated,' said Andrew, in an impromptu news conference.

Four days later Elizabeth revealed her feelings in her own way in a formal speech long-scheduled to mark the fortieth anniversary of her reign.

'1992 is not a year I shall look back on with undiluted pleasure,' she told the Prime Minister, the Leader of the Opposition, the Lord Mayor of the City of London and the assembled worthies gathered in the Guildhall for the lunch that was supposed to celebrate her forty years on the throne.

'In the words of one of my more sympathetic

correspondents,' she continued in a thin and shaky, Windsor-smoke-hoarsened voice, 'it has turned out to be an *annus horribilis*.'[†]

'One's Bum Year' was *The Sun's* earthy gloss on *annus* the next day. The Queen had had to use Latin to do it, but for the first time ever, she had given deliberate public voice to some genuine pain and vulnerability – and even an apology of sorts.

'No institution,' she declared bleakly, 'City, Monarchy, whatever – should expect to be free from the scrutiny of those who give it their loyalty and support, not to mention those who don't.'

This momentous portion of humble pie had been drafted by Sir Robert Fellowes, who had for some months been preparing an even greater act of humility – a proposal that the Queen should pay tax. Looking at the catastrophic impact of the young royals' misbehaviour on the standing of the monarchy, Fellowes decided the time had come to throw in the towel. Widespread household reforms by David Airlie, Elizabeth's forward-looking Lord Chamberlain, and a generous, long-term Civil List deal with Margaret Thatcher had finally put the royal finances on a solid footing. Elizabeth could actually afford to pay tax. But the Private Secretary knew the troubled history of the subject, and he had his arguments ready for battle when he took in his plan to the Queen.

'Robert was quite apprehensive,' recalled one of his colleagues.

In the event, Elizabeth yielded the point after the shortest of conversations. Confronted with the double audit of national opinion and of her own finances, she took 'just

---

† The phrase was not, in fact, proper Latin at all. *Annus horrendus* is the correct translation of horrible year. *Annus horribilis* was the more delightful and fanciful concoction of her 'sympathetic correspondent', former Assistant Private Secretary Sir Edward Ford, spoofing the title of John Dryden's poem, *Annus Mirabilis*, about the year 1665–6 which witnessed two naval victories over the Dutch and another fire – the Great Fire of London.

a matter of minutes' to agree to what had once seemed impossible – with only one condition. Fellowes must go down the road to Clarence House before the news became public to explain it to her mother.

'The drawing room was in shadow with very few lights on,' Fellowes related to William Shawcross twenty years later, recalling his 6.00 pm audience to convey the momentous news of the tax surrender to the Queen Mother. 'She gazed into the distance as I talked. When I finished there was a long pause, and then she said, "I think we'll have a drink."'

A few days later on 26th November 1992, John Major, recently chosen by the Conservatives to replace Margaret Thatcher as their leader and prime minister, rose in the Commons to announce that the Queen and the Prince of Wales would henceforward pay tax on their private incomes – and two weeks later he was on his feet again with news that the Prince and Princess of Wales had met with lawyers and had decided to separate.

Read together, the two announcements made clear why the Queen was forfeiting the privilege that her father and grandfather had fought so hard to protect. A thoroughly dutiful and virtuous monarch was having to pay the price of her children's bad behaviour.

In 1993 Elizabeth II started preparing for her first state visit to Russia. It had been a matter of Windsor principle not to visit the Soviet Union while it was ruled by successors to the Bolshevik regime that murdered the Romanovs. But now Russia had its first democratically elected leader in Boris Yeltsin.

One of the challenges the Queen had set herself since the days of Patrick Plunket was to come up with an original gift that would help break the ice of the potentially awkward blind date at the heart of every state visit. So what could

END OF THE TRIP.

Charles and Diana on their last royal tour together – to South Korea in November 1992. On 9ᵗʰ December they announced their separation

she give to Boris? The Foreign Office provided a clue; they discovered that the president's influential wife, Naina, loved gardening, and Elizabeth came up with the rest. She requested that the gardeners at Buckingham Palace harvest the seeds of their finest flowers, which she duly presented to the Yeltsins when they met in October 1994, all parcelled out in a delicate crystal set of drawers, complete with cultivation instructions.

'Oh, Borya,' exclaimed the delighted Naina Yeltsin. 'We can have our own Queen's garden out at the dacha!'

The Yeltsins returned the compliment with an album of rare Romanov letters and family photographs that gave Prince Philip lots to talk about – many of the pictures were of his tsarist relatives – while the new Russian leader discovered the comfort experienced by Britain's prime ministers in their weekly audiences: the chance to bend a sympathetic royal ear in absolute confidence. Elizabeth II had had some practice offering solace to beleaguered politicians, and Yeltsin poured his heart out to her, explaining the difficulties of corruption and violence in the new Russia and how difficult it was proving to establish decent government in the ruins of the old regime.

'Yes,' said the Queen as she listened supportively. 'You know, democracy takes a long time.'

The following spring found the Queen marking another pivotal moment, this time in South Africa where Nelson Mandela was the new president: the victor in April 1994 in the country's first ever fully democratic and non-racial election. In her forty-three years as Queen, some of this shy, restrained woman's warmest relationships had been with larger-than-life black African leaders. She had been closer, in certain ways, to ex-freedom fighters like Kenneth Kaunda and Jomo Kenyatta than she was to her middle-class Anglo-Saxon prime ministers. Maybe, as Mandela's biographer Anthony Sampson remarked, this had something to do with the naturalness with which these chieftains approached the totem of another tribe.

Born into a royal family himself, Mandela assembled no less than thirteen South African kings to meet Elizabeth II at the March 1995 state banquet in Capetown, where observers were struck by the relaxed rapport between the two heads of state.

'She's got a lot in common with him,' remarked one of her staff. 'You see, they've both spent a lot of time in prison.'

The Queen did not take offence when, in his letters, Mandela addressed her as 'Dear Elizabeth'. She liked the great man's simplicity. She had made her coming-of-age vow in South Africa, and in the fifty years since then she had stayed steadfast to the principles of fairness and equality that Mandela's triumph represented.

'On the apartheid issue she has always been on-side,' recalled her one-time Foreign Secretary, David Owen. 'It's the one-man, one-vote principle. On racial matters she is absolutely colour-blind.'

The historic success of Elizabeth II's royal tours provided a riposte to the critics who suggested that the misconduct of her children reflected poorly on her abilities as a mother. Since 1949 she had been a working mother – the most working mother of all, in fact, from the point of view of Britain, the other nations of the Commonwealth and any other nation who had dealings with the intriguing figure of the Queen. That sort of mothering was her job, and she had done it consummately well.

6

As your Queen and as a grandmother
1995–2012

The Queen had hoped that Charles and Diana's legal separation would stop their feuding, but the rivalry between them ran too deep. Desperate to counter his wife's media popularity, Charles worked through 1993 with the broadcaster Jonathan Dimbleby to produce a film and a book that would restore his reputation – and achieved the very opposite result.

'Did you try,' asked Dimbleby in the TV film that was broadcast at the end of June 1994 to an audience of 14 million in Britain alone, 'to be faithful and honourable to your wife when you took the vow of marriage?'

'Yes,' replied Charles, 'until it became irretrievably broken down, us both having tried.'

Charles described Camilla as his 'friend for a very long time,' and the next day Dimbleby confirmed that the infidelity to which the Prince referred had indeed occurred with Mrs Parker Bowles.

'The boy was off his head,' growled a canny, long-term confidant of both the Queen and the Queen Mother.

For Charles to confess adultery from his own mouth shattered one of the fundamental underpinnings of the monarchical edifice, the subconscious belief that royal people, like one's parents, do not actually 'do' things like that, any more than they go to the lavatory. At a stroke, a million maiden aunts were robbed of their comforting illusion that royal folk magically adhere to a higher standard, and that lurid tales of Charles's misconduct – not to mention the terrible 'Tampax tape' – had been 'all got up by the papers.' Following the public announcement of his cuckolding by the man he had courteously continued to treat as his friend, the hitherto patient Colonel Andrew Parker Bowles finally sued for divorce.

For Elizabeth, the sting came in the thick 620-page biography that Dimbleby published later that year with Charles's approval, painstakingly listing his grievances against his parents and stigmatising Elizabeth as a bad mother. The Queen said nothing to her son directly, but Anne, Andrew and Edward were furious at their brother's disloyalty and said so to his face.

There were few people in any of the palaces who did not deplore Charles and Dimbleby's effort, with Diana at the top of the list. In 620 pages her husband had done full credit to the Princess's tantrums, self-absorption and collusion with the press, though the book's most profoundly hurtful revelation actually confirmed the nub of Diana's case, that Charles had never really loved her. Dimbleby left no doubt that although Charles had proposed to Diana through a sense of duty and a wish 'to do the right thing for this country and for my family,' his heart had actually been committed all along to Camilla, for whom he felt a 'deep friendship that could properly be described as "love".'

'I'll get my own back on him,' Diana vowed to her staff with relish. 'Just you wait and see. I will get my revenge.'

On 20th November 1995 over 23 million British viewers, the BBC's highest rating ever, watched Diana nervously but deftly outgun Charles as she answered the questions of Martin Bashir, a young reporter on the BBC's flagship current affairs programme, *Panorama*.

'There were three of us in this marriage,' was her edgy skewering of the Camilla situation, and when it came to her own infidelity she carefully skipped around the suggestion of 'adultery' with its Old Testament and divorce court grimness, tiptoeing lightly into the meadow of romance.

'Yes, I adored him,' she said of Major James Hewitt. 'Yes, I was in love with him. But I was very let down.'

Twenty-three million hearts went out to her – particularly among her already overflowing constituency of women who knew a man who had done them wrong.

The most important woman watching the interview, however, was not impressed. The Queen had taken Diana's side from the earliest days, and particularly in the division of roles after the separation when she had resisted her son's efforts to cut down his wife's access to royal perks like the Queen's Flight and the royal train.

'His people pushed very hard,' remembers one of the Princess's advisers. 'But the Queen wasn't having it. She insisted that Diana should have her dignity and her rights.'

Diana's *Panorama* broadcast, however, changed the Queen's thinking – how could she accept her daughter-in-law going out to represent the family after such a personal attack? Diana had strayed into dangerous constitutional territory when she questioned Charles's fitness to be king – 'My wish is that my husband finds peace of mind, and from that follow other things.' And her most quotable quote, following a series of comments about the need for the monarchy to have 'more contact with its people' could even be interpreted as Diana's direct challenge to Elizabeth herself: 'I'd like to be a queen of people's hearts.'

The Queen of the United Kingdom acted at last. The previous December had seen the second anniversary of the couple's legal separation, the moment when British law permitted a simple no-fault divorce by mutual consent. Princess Margaret, who had divorced promptly on her two-year deadline, felt strongly that Charles should do the same.

'Do it straight away,' she told her nephew and, seeing his eyes glaze over at advice he had clearly heard before, she kicked him sharply on the knee.

'What's that for?' he asked.

'Shape up,' she said.

On 20th December 1995, a uniformed courier from Windsor Castle delivered a personal letter from the Queen to her daughter-in-law. 'Dearest Diana,' it began, according to Paul Burrell, Diana's butler and 'Rock'* in her days of separation, to whom she showed the letter. Elizabeth explained that she had been discussing the 'sad and complicated situation' with the Archbishop of Canterbury and the Prime Minister, who were both agreed, and she was now expressing her own personal wish that Charles and Diana should formally and finally divorce 'in the best interests of the country.' She ended the note with an affectionate scribble, 'Love from Mama', but her message brooked no argument.

There was money to sort out, the joint custody of the children, which was amicably settled, and the question of titles. Could Diana remain an HRH? The Palace was horrified by how much Diana demanded – £17 million – while Diana professed herself 'destroyed' that she would no longer be a Royal Highness (the Palace insisted fiercely that the Princess had initially offered to surrender the title in a personal meeting with the Queen).

It took six months of haggling, but in the end both sides got what they wanted. For Elizabeth it was crucial that the title of His or Her Royal Highness, which merits a bow or a curtsey, should remain the personal gift of the monarch denoting a direct family connection with the Crown, while Diana wanted her freedom, which £17 million could give her and which the HRH did not.

The dream marriage formally came to an end on 28th August 1996 with the granting of a decree absolute. Charles, Diana and the monarchy could all now make a fresh start.

---

* According to Burrell, Diana told the former footman, 'You are my rock.' According to a cherished royal joke, what Diana actually said to Burrell was, 'You're wearing my frock.'

But just one year and three days later, the British ambassador in Paris rang Balmoral around 1.00 am, rousing the duty Private Secretary, Robin Janvrin, from his sleep. The embassy was receiving police reports, he said, of a serious car crash that involved the Princess of Wales.

The news of Diana's death came through from Paris just before 4.00 am, and the Queen's first reaction was to think of her grandsons.

'We must get the radios out of their rooms,' she said to Charles.

Mother and son discussed whether to wake William and Harry – their grandmother felt strongly that they should have a decent night's rest before they had to face what would be the most difficult day of their lives. 'Looking after the boys' became her top priority in the difficult days that lay ahead.

'We must get them out and away from the television,' she said as she clicked across the mournful images of the dead Princess being run non-stop on every television channel. 'Let's get them both up in the hills.'

She assigned Peter Phillips, Princess Anne's bluff rugby-playing son, the task of taking William and Harry out on the moors on stalking and fishing expeditions, with lots of mucking around on the brothers' noisy scramble motorbikes. At fifteen, William seemed to take it bravely, on the outside at least. Not quite thirteen, Harry had been more obviously upset. 'Was everyone quite sure that Mummy was dead?' he was heard to enquire. Could it just be checked to make sure there had not been some mistake?

Elizabeth had no doubt that the calming and secluded Highlands were the best place in the world to help the boys with the therapy that always lifted her in times of trouble – lots of fresh air and exercise. But down in London there was mutiny in the air.

'Where is the Queen when the country needs her?' demanded an open letter on the front page of *The Sun*. 'She is 550 miles from London, the focal point of the nation's grief ... Every hour the palace remains empty adds to the public anger at what they perceive to be a snub to the People's Princess.'

'The People's Princess' was the phrase coined on the morning of Diana's death by Tony Blair, Elizabeth's new Prime Minister, in an emotional speech on his way to church in his Sedgefield constituency in Durham. Blair's centrist and recast 'New' Labour party had won power the previous May with a massive majority, with no little thanks to their leader's uncanny instinct for the public mood. But now the 'People's Princess' caught the national mood a little too sharply, setting the emotional, 'let it all hang out' spirit of Diana in contrast to the stoic but also stony-faced Royal Family, who had gone to church that Sunday saying nothing and emerging to the world dry-eyed.

'No Mention of Accident,' ran the reproachful headline of *The Times* reporting the decision of the Balmoral chaplain to say special prayers for Charles and his sons, but to make no reference at all to Diana or those who died with her, the French chauffeur Henri Paul and her Egyptian boyfriend Dodi Fayed.

Compounding the Queen's absence from London was the lack of any flag flying at half mast above Buckingham Palace as a sign of royal mourning. Over the years the tradition had developed that the Royal Standard, the personal coat of arms of the monarch, should fly over the palace to denote the royal presence, and that no other flag should fly in her absence. As people queued in the Mall to sign the official condolence books and lay their own tribute on the mounds of flowers growing against the palace railings they looked up at the bare flagpole with disbelief and increasing anger. It made for compulsive television.

'I've just been watching Sky News ...' warned Blair's PR

guru Alastair Campbell in a phone call to Robert Fellowes. 'I think they're going to make some mischief over this thing of the flag.'

'I hear what you're saying ...' replied the Private Secretary. 'But I'm not sure it's going to be as easy as it looks to please the public on this one.'

This was Fellowes' way of saying that he knew his boss, and that he doubted there was any way on earth he could persuade the Queen to be flexible over the flag. It was a matter of tradition, and he knew very well how tradition was Elizabeth's fallback position onto something greater than herself. It could be compared to how non-royal people feel at their children's Christmas carol concert or when the bugle sounds on Remembrance Day – the tingle of nobler things.

Tradition was one of the keystones of the royal mystery. If Prince Charles had died in a car crash the previous Sunday, the Queen would not now be flying the Union Jack at half mast over Buckingham Palace. She had not done it for her beloved father. She would not expect it for herself or for her mother. So why should tradition be overturned for a young woman who, just like Uncle David, had put her own wayward concerns before those of the family and had become the focus of such trouble and divisiveness?

Fellowes tried making the argument, but got the answer he expected. Both Elizabeth and her husband had a deep mistrust of making concessions to the popular concerns of the moment, particularly when voiced by the tabloid media.

'It's like feeding Christians to the lions,' explained a former royal press secretary. 'It just makes the lions roar for more.'

Unhappiness over the flag was something that the sacred and enduring monarchy should rise above in a world of trendy gestures. The flagpole must stay bare.

'There were times in that week,' said a No. 10 insider, 'when you could not believe what was coming down the line from Balmoral. You wondered if they were living in the same century.'

By the Wednesday following Diana's death there were people in Buckingham Palace who were feeling the same.

'When the Queen was at Buckingham Palace or Windsor,' said a former adviser trying to explain the Queen's obstinacy over the flag, 'she was psychologically much more prepared to get involved with something unexpected. But her time relaxing in Scotland was so precious to her ... She was not thrilled when prime ministers or Privy Councils or something interrupted "her Balmoral".'

Elizabeth had been encouraging this sense of detachment for the sake of her grandsons. But what worked for William and Harry was disastrous when it came to the Queen's own willingness to take on board the messages coming from London – most of them conveyed via the courtly Robin Janvrin, a former naval officer and diplomat.

'Robin had a tough job up there,' remembers one of the London team. 'We were all coming off the street as it were, with our feeling of what was happening out on the ground. Then he had to walk down the corridor, a delegation of one, and convince the family – the Queen, Prince Philip, Prince Charles – all gathered in the sitting room, that there was a crisis and they couldn't just look at it in the traditional family way. Robin's a diplomat, a conciliator, and then he was still relatively junior. It was very easy for Prince Philip to overrule him – "What's all the fuss about? It will calm down."'

When Janvrin was rebuffed, Robert Fellowes would pick up the phone in the palace and go into action.

'I love Robert – he's incredibly brave,' says one of his former colleagues. 'If he believes in something, he'll go right over the top fighting for it, whatever the cost.'

The cost proved painful for Fellowes himself and for several other senior courtiers in a series of deeply wounding confrontations with the Queen and with Prince Philip. By the end of 'D+3', as they called Wednesday 3rd September 1997 in their military-style command meetings, the Queen's advisers were unanimous. There must be some compromise over the flag, as well as some drastic change in the timetable decision that had been taken by Elizabeth and her husband at the start of the week – that they would not show their faces in London until the morning of the funeral, coming down overnight on the royal train, then heading straight back to Scotland afterwards. Such a fleeting visit to the capital would only increase the accusations of indifference and heartlessness that were now being hurled openly at the Royal Family.

But the Queen and her husband refused to budge. They both got angry with their advisers, and in an ugly fashion. When the memory of those desperate hours and what was said at Balmoral comes up today, all those involved go silent and refuse to describe what transpired. They had seen a side of Elizabeth II that they would evidently prefer to forget.

'A lot of people,' recalls one of them, 'were heavily scarred by it.'

D+4, Thursday 4th September 1997, dawned bright and clear in Balmoral. The weather across Britain during the week following Diana's death was marked by extraordinary warmth and sunshine. But that was not the tone of the newspapers waiting on Elizabeth's breakfast table.

'Show us you care!' demanded the *Express* over a photo of a flinty-faced Queen. The newspapers had scoured their archives for images of Elizabeth II at her grimmest, grumpiest and most double-chinned.

'Your people are suffering,' proclaimed the *Mirror*. 'Speak to us, Ma'am!'

As usual, it was the Murdoch press that most menacingly evoked the tumbrils.

'Let Charles and William and Harry weep together in the lonely Scottish Highlands,' said *The Sun*. 'We can understand that. But the Queen's place is with her people. She should fly back to London immediately.'

Down in London, Elizabeth's team, now joined by her Press Secretary Geoffrey Crawford, who had been in Australia, digested the revolutionary onslaught. They spoke on the phone to Robin Janvrin in Balmoral, and then moved into their daily 10.00 am meeting with the Lord Chamberlain's committee that was arranging the details of the ceremony on Saturday. Afterwards they got back on the speakerphone with Janvrin, who was now joined by the Queen, and in the course of just forty-five minutes they totally recast the shape of the next forty-eight hours. The previous day's battles over the flagpole were quite ignored.

'The Queen has ruthless common sense,' says one of her private secretaries. 'She has the ability to move on. If you can explain clearly why something has to be done, and she agrees, that's the end of the matter.'

Elizabeth's battling the previous day had been on behalf of the timelessness of the monarchy, as she saw it. Now she bent to a principle that was even more timeless – her need to stay in business.

'A monarchy which ignores the people,' says one of her aides, 'has no function and cannot survive.'

Was it the morning headlines, or a change of heart in the night? Either way, Elizabeth accepted that her stiff upper lip would now have to soften – and the details of the wobbling were set in place at once. A phone call instructed the Balmoral pastor to arrange a service that very evening at which the name of Diana *would* be mentioned. Afterwards the Royal Family would get out of their cars to inspect the flowers that had been laid at the castle gates, and the next day the entire family – the boys included – would fly down early to London so they could do the same and talk to people outside the London palaces. The royal train was cancelled, two RAF planes were lined up and the BBC was told to set up its cameras inside Buckingham Palace: Her Majesty would be making an eve-of-funeral broadcast to the nation.

The turn-around was incredible – cynical or finally realistic, depending on your point of view. In just forty-five minutes Elizabeth II had backtracked, adapted and totally reinvented her role in Diana's ending, moving herself from the margin to the very centre of the drama. Now redemption hinged on her ability to accomplish what she liked least and did worst – expressing her feelings and speaking on television.

At 3.00 pm on D+5, Friday 5th September 1997, the atmosphere was tense and frantic in the Chinese Drawing Room in Buckingham Palace, from which Elizabeth II was due to record her address to the nation in less than two hours. The hastily rigged circuit of lamps and electrical connections was audibly 'buzzing' and Peter Edwards, the Queen's long-serving sound technician, could not get a clear track on his tape.

The Queen had just arrived at the palace with her husband, stopping outside to inspect the huge mounds of flowers piled up against the railings.

'Would you like me to place them for you?' she asked a little girl who handed her a bunch of five red roses.

'No, Your Majesty,' replied the girl. 'They are for you.'

People in the crowd began to clap.

Edwards had been told the Queen would be recording her 'piece to camera' around 4.00 or 4.30, to go out later on the evening news, but Robert Fellowes and Geoffrey Crawford were hatching other plans.

'It was a psychological thing,' explains one aide. 'She goes flat when she knows it's being recorded. When she knows it's real, she rises to the challenge.'

The Queen's only previous 'address to the nation' in 1991, on the eve of the Gulf War, had been recorded, and then broadcast 'as live' a few minutes later. It had been adequate by traditional standards, but plain vanilla. Today, Crawford and Fellowes decided, they would have to put their boss on her mettle, and they walked together to the Belgian Suite at the back of the palace where she was having tea with her husband.

'Do you think you can do it?' Fellowes asked the Queen.

'If that's what I've got to do,' she replied.

Elizabeth looked through her script one last time and suggested some final alterations. Fellowes went to his office to get the changes transcribed, while Crawford walked back to Edwards and the studio staff. There were just ninety minutes left before transmission.

'Can we do it live?' asked the Press Secretary.

BBC riggers scrambled as they ran sweating up and down the stairs, running the leads to connect with the outside broadcasting production trucks.

'Are you sure you can say every word in this speech and really believe it?' someone had asked Elizabeth during the drafting process.

'Certainly,' she replied. 'I believe every word.'

At 5.40 she did a final run-through with the autocue, looking into the camera as Fellowes and Crawford watched. One rehearsal was enough, they decided. Then at 5.55 the countdown started, with the two monitors in the corner showing different pictures – the live feed of BBC programming leading up to the news, and the interior palace shot of the Queen staring intently into the lens.

'Five, four, three, two,' counted the floor manager, and then motioned to Elizabeth, mouthing 'Go!' The two pictures became one.

'Since last Sunday's dreadful news,' began the Queen, 'we have seen an overwhelming expression of sadness at Diana's death … It is not easy to express a sense of loss, since the initial shock is often succeeded by a mixture of other

SEA OF FLOWERS.
*The Queen and Prince Philip inspect the floral tributes to Diana outside
Buckingham Palace. 5ᵗʰ September 1997*

feelings – disbelief, incomprehension, anger and concern for those who remain. We have all felt those emotions in these last few days. So what I say to you now as your Queen, and as a grandmother, I say from my heart.'

Fellowes had drafted the speech down in London, working with Crawford and the Lord Chamberlain, David Airlie, and with the Queen and Robin Janvrin who were up in Balmoral. The almost final version had been faxed to Downing Street, and it was Alastair Campbell who suggested the magic phrase that struck a chord with every watcher and listener.

'Alastair was quite tentative about it,' recalls one palace insider. 'He said, "The Prime Minister has only one comment ... would it be right for the Queen to say *speaking as a grandmother?*" We grabbed it and used it.'

The other masterstroke was the live exterior backdrop

behind the Queen as she spoke, so viewers could look out over her shoulders through the palace window at the mourners who were coming and going. Peter Edwards had been struggling all afternoon to get an uncluttered soundtrack, and the decision to go live had made his problem worse.

'Can't you get a clearer sound?' the BBC control room was shouting down the line.

Edwards opened the window to get a few minutes of fresh air, and heard an extraordinary noise – the murmuring of ten thousand or more people as they milled around in the traffic-free area outside the palace.

'It was a sound of its own,' he remembers, 'like nothing I'd quite heard before. This was London. *Then*. At that very particular moment. I shivered when I heard it.'

Edwards stationed a microphone outside to pick up the shuffle of the crowds, blending it into the audio track from the Queen's own microphone. The electronic interference was masked, and the living, brooding noise of her people mingled directly with what she was saying.

'This week in Balmoral we have all been trying to help William and Harry come to terms with the devastating loss that they and the rest of us have suffered … I hope that tomorrow we can all, wherever we are, join in expressing our grief for Diana's loss and her all-too-short life. It is a chance to show to the whole world the British nation united in grief and respect. May those who died rest in peace and may we, each and every one of us, thank God for someone who made many, many people happy.'

A snappier ending might have been to thank God for someone who had 'made us all' happy. But Elizabeth knew that was not true, and the strength of her words was that they did not flirt with exaggerated or false sentiment. She had searched her heart – the key, emotional word she had used at the beginning of the speech – and although her reservations were there for those who cared to look for them, so were the good things that she saw in Diana.

'AS YOUR QUEEN AND AS A GRANDMOTHER.'
Elizabeth II broadcasts live from the Chinese Drawing Room, Buckingham Palace.
5th September 1997

'She's turned it around!' exclaimed Arthur Edwards, *The Sun's* royal photographer who had retired to a pub to watch the broadcast on television. 'It brought a lump to my throat. "Thank God," I thought. "She's back in charge."'

Elizabeth II had taken her time about it but, when it really mattered, she had done her job. She had managed to express genuine emotion and she had also acknowledged, through her willingness to change her plans and to make her speech, that she listened to her people – that her subjects, in fact, were ultimately her boss.

Britain's emotional reaction to the death of Diana was diagnosed at the time as a very modern type of collective nervous breakdown. But a gun carriage rolling slowly, young princes marching with their heads bowed, and choral music in the Abbey (with a little help from Elton John) provided a set of remedies for the national trauma that were essentially traditional.

'I for one,' Elizabeth had said in her live broadcast, 'believe that there are lessons to be drawn from her life and from the extraordinary and moving reaction to her death.'

She proved as good as her word.

'After the broadcast,' says one of her advisers, 'we found it easier to convince her about doing things. She listened to us more, and was just a little more prepared to take risks.'

When the Queen visited a school before Diana's death, she would stand at the doorway and stay on her feet. Now she was prepared to go in and sit down among the children – and even, in one French language class, to show off a little of her immaculate French. In one Australian outback school she took questions from the class, cheerfully admitting she had no idea how many rooms there were in Buckingham Palace.

But she warned her staff against taking informality too far.

'No stunts,' she would say. 'I am not a politician.'

She was positively annoyed when the press interpreted her 'new informality' as the 'Diana effect'.

'Don't they realise I've done it before?' she asked, looking at the morning press digest. 'I've done *everything* before.'

'The Way Ahead' Group was a joint family and Palace attempt to learn from past mistakes. Every six months, the Queen, her husband, their children and their advisors met to sort out problems like flag protocol – whenever the Queen was not in residence, it was decided, a Union Jack would now fly over Buckingham Palace. There would be no more bare flagpoles. And they also looked to the future.

NOT AMUSED.

The Queen holds hands with Tony Blair (right, Cherie Blair) at the Millennium Celebrations at the Dome in London. 31ˢᵗ December 1999

The succession rules should be altered, they proposed, so that girls were no longer disadvantaged – the first child born of either sex should succeed. A dozen years later that change would finally make its way into the statute books of all sixteen realms in which Elizabeth reigned, together with a repeal of the old 18th century ban on heirs marrying a Roman Catholic.

As the world changed, Elizabeth II breasted the waves with her dry and rather mordant sense of humour. Talking to a youthful couple at a Buckingham Palace garden party, she was quite unfazed when the girl's mobile telephone rang to the young woman's agonised embarrassment.

'You'd better answer that,' said the Queen without blinking. 'It might be someone important.'

On 11th September 2001, four years and just a few days after Diana's death, Elizabeth II was once again staring at a television, transfixed, like millions of viewers around the world, by a foreign tragedy that she could not believe was happening – and since it was September, she was once again at Balmoral. This time, however, the royal reactions were more responsive. Within hours of the twin towers being hit, a message of sympathy had gone to President George W. Bush and plans were under way for the Queen's return to London for a service in St Paul's.

'These days,' said a courtier, 'everyone is really on their toes.'

11th September 2001 was also the day when 'Porchie', Lord Carnarvon – aged seventy-seven, the son of an American mother and married for forty-five years to an American wife – died while watching his television.

'Grief is the price we pay for love,' was the curiously personal sentiment with which the Queen chose to end the message read out in her name at a Washington memorial service for those who died on 9/11, and the words only made sense if she herself was mourning someone she had loved. She had spoken to Porchie or gone racing with him almost every afternoon of her adult life. He was the hotline to the gossip she enjoyed most of all: which mares were in foal, what young stock looked promising. He would ring her from the sale-rooms when he was buying on her behalf, holding up the phone so she could hear the bidding. The pair of them did not produce Prince Andrew together, as malicious rumour suggested, but they did produce countless classy racehorses and over fifty years of memories and very happy afternoons, which all ended suddenly on 9/11. There were tears in the Queen's eyes as she left St Paul's Cathedral after the service of remembrance on 14th September 2001.

Five months later, in February 2002, she welcomed one of the American heroes of 9/11, Mayor Rudolph Giuliani, to Buckingham Palace to line up with the brave British soldiers, policemen, social workers and other distinguished citizens invited to the palace to receive their medals, ribbons or – in Giuliani's case – an honorary knighthood† at one of the royal investitures. There are twenty-five or so of these ceremonies held every year and Elizabeth once remarked that, of all the different aspects of her job, she considered investitures the most important.

She does her homework thoroughly. On the previous weekend she goes away, usually to Windsor, with a briefing list containing several paragraphs on each of the individuals who are due to be honoured. She reads the briefing thoroughly to find out what each district nurse or charity worker has done to earn their award, and picks out a few key words for each person. This list is given to her equerry, who then whispers the key words as each recipient approaches the crimson dais in the palace ballroom.

The key words prompt the personal question that the Queen has prepared just for you, and if you give her a shortish, intelligent answer, she will ask you another. If you offer a petrified stare or can only talk gibberish, she will put you out of your misery with a quick smile of farewell.

'It was lovely,' recipients regularly say to court officials. 'We chatted for several minutes.'

In fact, nobody gets more than thirty seconds. Elizabeth II processes her prize-givings at the rate of five recipients every two minutes – up to one hundred and thirty people in an hour and ten minutes. Then off to lunch.

Traditionally, she has met her people's elected head of government in an audience before dinner every Tuesday evening, and her latest prime ministers have reported the same experiences of comfort and support as their predecessors.

---

† The Mayor of New York was invested as a Knight of the Order of the British Empire – Sir Rudolph Giuliani KBE. Since the US constitution prohibits its citizens from holding any foreign title or dignity, however, Giuliani accepted the knighthood in a purely honorary sense, following the example of such Americans as Sir Billy Graham, Sir Bill Gates, Sir Steven Spielberg, Sir Henry Kissinger, Sir Colin Powell and Sir Ronald Reagan. Non-US honorary knights include Sir Shimon Peres, Sir Pelé and Sir Bono.

'Nobody else is present,' recalled John Major fondly. 'Except for the occasional corgi.'

'It's the one regular thing he does that he really looks forward to,' said Alastair Campbell, speaking of Tony Blair in 2001. 'After a while, everything in the diary can become a bit of a chore, but it's one fixture where you never hear him saying "Oh God!"'

'It's just the two of you,' said her twelfth and youngest Prime Minister, David Cameron, talking to Robert Hardman of his experiences since 2010, 'so you can say exactly what you like, and she can ask what she likes.'

James Callaghan cleverly noted the delusion of every British premier, that the Queen dealt with him or her 'in a much more friendly way' than with their predecessor. 'I am sure that is not true,' he remarked. 'Sunny Jim', who knew a thing or two about generating the appearance of geniality, pointed out that whatever her prime ministers might imagine that the Queen was offering them personally, it was not friendship. 'It is friendliness.'

In 2006, movie-goers around the world were treated to a cinematic version of the private prime ministerial audience as depicted in *The Queen*, Peter Morgan's Oscar-winning dramatisation of the crisis that followed the death of Diana. The imagined relationship between Elizabeth II (Helen Mirren) and Tony Blair (Michael Sheen) lay at the heart of the drama and, when the film appeared to great acclaim, Blair (in Downing Street for more than ten years, second only in tenure to Margaret Thatcher) was still in office.

'I understand there's a film out,' said the Queen at their next audience, pausing briefly and giving him a meaningful look. 'I shan't be seeing it.'

Her prime minister did not miss a beat.

'I shan't be either,' said Tony Blair – and he says he still hasn't.

PAST AND PRESENT.
*Elizabeth II's latest prime minister, David Cameron, leads the
Queen past photographs of his predecessors in Downing Street.
Top row from left: Edward Heath (1970–74), Margaret Thatcher (1979–90),
and Tony Blair (1997–2007).
Bottom row from left: Harold Wilson (1964–70 and 1974–76), James Callaghan
(1976–79) and, mostly obscured, Gordon Brown (2007–2010).
Rear right, Samantha Cameron. 21ˢᵗ June 2011*

On the morning of 30th March 2002, Easter Saturday, just
a few weeks before her seventy-sixth birthday, Elizabeth II
was taking one of her favourite forms of exercise, riding on
horseback in Windsor Great Park, when the detective on the
horse behind her received a call. The royal doctors had just
visited Royal Lodge where the Queen Mother, now in her
hundred and second year, had been ailing for some time.
They reckoned she would not outlast the day.

Elizabeth was at her mother's bedside when she died
peacefully that afternoon. With her were Sarah Chatto and

FUNERAL OF PRINCESS MARGARET.
The Queen with her sister's children Viscount Linley and Sarah Chatto outside St George's Chapel, Windsor. 15ᵗʰ February 2002

David Linley, the children of Princess Margaret who had died only a few weeks earlier, after several years of pain, strokes and depression. The Princess had been cremated at her own request. She wanted the urn with her ashes to rest beside her father's coffin in King George VI Memorial Chapel at Windsor, and there she was joined, on 9th April 2002, by the casket of her mother.

It was almost deliberate, the graceful way in which Elizabeth's mother faded from the scene, as if the older Queen Elizabeth did not want to overshadow her daughter's Golden Jubilee, the marking of fifty years since her 1952 accession, that was due to be celebrated later that summer. The Queen had always been content to live and reign in the shadow of her flamboyant and extrovert 'Mummy', generously funding her extravagances from footmen and champagne to the racetrack.

FAREWELL GLANCE.
Elizabeth II escorts the coffin of her mother out of Westminster Abbey with Princes William, Edward, Charles and Harry. 9ᵗʰ April 2002

'Really,' she once remarked happily, 'what with my mother and her racehorses and my mother-in-law with her nunneries ...'‡

With the disappearance of her mother and sister as well as of Diana – chronic upstagers all three of them – the unassuming Elizabeth could finally take her place as mother of the nation.

'Act 1 good. Act 2 bad,' is how one of her former private secretaries sums up her reign. The Golden Jubilee of 2002 provided a brighter start to Act 3, which was celebrated in London with a rock concert for 12,000 members of the public

---

‡ Prince Philip's mother, the beautiful and congenitally deaf Princess Alice of Battenberg, (1885–1969) founded a Greek Orthodox nursing order of nuns, the Christian Sisterhood of Martha and Mary. She gave away all her money and lived her final years as a guest of the Queen in Buckingham Palace. She is buried in Jerusalem in recognition of her work saving Jewish refugees in wartime Greece.

in Buckingham Palace gardens while Brian May of Queen plucked out 'God Save the Queen' with his electric guitar on the palace roof. The monarchy went pop – and multi-racial too. A wholly non-military pageant in the Mall was kicked off by an array of gospel choirs that demonstrated one of the success stories of the reign – the largely peaceful shifting of the country's ethnic mix. The Empire had come home.

There were signs of a shift too up on the palace balcony, where the Queen, Prince Philip and their children occupied centre stage, but where public interest and the long lenses of the press now focused on the new generation: Princess Anne's children Peter and Zara Phillips (twenty-four and twenty-one), Prince Andrew's daughters Beatrice (thirteen) and Eugenie (twelve) and, in particular, on the tragic and intriguing sons of Charles and Diana – William (nearly twenty and just completing his first year at St Andrews University), and Harry (seventeen years old and about to start his final year at Eton).

Elizabeth II may have had her failings as a mother, but she more than compensated in the way that she grandmothered her semi-orphaned grandsons, in particular the future King William V. Charles, like his brothers Andrew and Edward, had been packed off to Gordonstoun, his father's old school in the wilds of northern Scotland, where he had been bullied without respite. He and Diana were agreed that Eton, just over the river from Windsor, was the college for William, and Elizabeth was delighted.

When their diaries allowed it, 4.00 on Sunday afternoon became a high spot of the week for both the Queen and her grandson. William took the short walk over the bridge and up to the castle for tea. When he was a baby, Elizabeth had crawled around the floor with him. As he grew older she had taken him riding. Now she talked about her grandson's water polo and his rugby games and shared the details of her own life – the blue boxes with the dispatches from the Foreign Office, the red boxes, the investiture briefing lists, the objectives of her next tour or state visit and the meaning of ceremonies like the annual gathering of Garter Knights, the supreme order of chivalry that William himself would head one day.

'Her idea,' explains one of her private secretaries, 'was to encourage his sense of destiny and to give him a sense of what his role would be.'

William needed little encouragement. He was thrilled to handle a document sealed by Henry VIII, or to pore with his grandmother over a letter written by Queen Victoria to Benjamin Disraeli.

'There's no question you can ask [that] she won't already know about,' Prince William told Robert Hardman in 2011. 'She's very up for that sort of thing. And for me particularly, being the young bloke coming through, being able to talk to my grandmother and ask her questions and know there's sound advice coming back is very reassuring.'

It is more and more through 'the young bloke coming through' that Elizabeth II is now getting the job done. By the jubilee celebrations of 2002 William had already met Catherine Middleton, his fellow history of art student at St Andrews University, and his grandmother played an important role in the process by which the couple were able to live together – 'in sin' by the standards that once applied – for the best part of nine years before they married. By the time Prince Andrew got engaged to Sarah Ferguson in 1986, Elizabeth had already abandoned the 'bedded-can't-be-wedded' principle that had wrought such havoc with the middle years of her reign, and she had taken the process a stage further with her youngest son Edward, providing his girlfriend Sophie Rhys-Jones with a bedroom close to his in Buckingham Palace.

'Contrary to popular opinion, we've never lived together,' Sophie primly declared on their engagement day in January 1999, proving that she had a contempt for the nation's intelligence to match that of her fiancé.

Her future mother-in-law was more realistic. When *The Sun* revealed in 1989 that it was in possession of steamy love letters written by the Queen's equerry, Commander Timothy Laurence, to her daughter Princess Anne, still married at that date to Mark Phillips, opinion in the royal household was censorious.

'There was much talk of high treason for Tim committing adultery with the Princess,' remembers one courtier who rather liked the quiet and serious Laurence. 'I think one of the few people who weren't shocked was the Queen. She liked her equerry [who would marry Princess Anne in 1992 after her divorce from Mark Phillips], and I think she took the view that if the Princess found some satisfaction in her relationship with him, that was not a bad thing. "I've decided," she said, "that I'm not stuffy enough for my age."'

That proved to be the Queen's unstuffy opinion when she learned that William had 'moved in' with Kate up at St Andrews, where a royal detective shared lodgings with the couple and, unofficially, kept an eye on the security of both. Later, like Prince Charles, the Queen was quite relaxed with the idea that Kate should effectively shack up with William in London at Clarence House – or, if she had any reservations, she decided to keep them to herself. As the young Prince later put it in another context, 'She won't necessarily force advice on you. She'll let you work it out for yourself.'

The Queen could not be so relaxed, however, when it came to her eldest son and Camilla Parker Bowles. One day late in the 1990s Sir Robin Janvrin was waiting for a meeting with Prince Charles's staff in St James's Palace, when the Prince's Private Secretary, Stephen Lamport, sauntered in.

'We have Mrs Parker Bowles here,' said Lamport casually, 'and the Prince of Wales wondered if you would like to come up for a drink with her?'

'Certainly not,' responded the startled Janvrin, springing out of his chair. He could not possibly meet Mrs Parker

NEW CHAPTER.
HELLO! *Magazine celebrates the wedding of Charles and Camilla. 9th April 2005*

Bowles without the express permission of the Queen – and that remained the position for Elizabeth's staff until the couple finally got married in April 2005. As Supreme Governor of the Church of England, the Queen had to abide by the church's refusal to marry couples whose adultery was a factor in the breakdown of their original marriages, and she, with the Duke of Edinburgh, declined to attend the couple's registry office marriage in Windsor Guildhall.

Later that afternoon she emerged smiling broadly on the steps of St George's Chapel inside Windsor Castle, where the couple had been through a service of blessing at which they both acknowledged and 'bewailed' to the Archbishop of Canterbury their 'manifold sins and wickedness which ... [they], from time to time, most grievously ... [had] committed.' Perhaps for Elizabeth II this was finally the end of the long and embarrassing drama of Act 2.

Shortly afterwards, a significant tweaking was made to the family order of precedence. Normally the wife of the Prince of Wales is the second lady in the land, but for family occasions, it was announced, Camilla would now be ranked fourth, after the Queen, the Princess Royal (Princess Anne) and Elizabeth's cousin, Princess Alexandra of Kent. Out of deference to Diana's memory, furthermore, Camilla would henceforward be known as Duchess of Rothesay when in Scotland and Duchess of Cornwall when south of the border, taking her style from Charles's ducal titles. She was finally married to her Prince, but she would never be known as the Princess of Wales.

On 10th June 2011, the Queen helped Prince Philip celebrate his ninetieth birthday, and the British press joined in merrily, giving credit to 'The Duke' for social initiatives like his award scheme for young people, but principally celebrating his proficiency at what he himself called 'Dontopedalogy – the science of opening your mouth and putting your foot in it.'

Many of the tributes were simply lists ('Ninety gaffes in ninety years'), running from Philip's greeting to the

Paraguayan dictator Alfredo Stroessner – 'what a pleasant change to be in a country that isn't run by its people' – to his compliment to the singer Tom Jones at the Royal Variety Show in 1969 – 'What do you gargle with? Pebbles?'

Encountering fellow Brits on foreign tours had inspired some of his classics – 'You've not managed to get eaten yet?' (Papua New Guinea, 1998), 'You can't have been here long – you haven't got a pot belly' (Hungary, 1993) and, most famous of all, 'If you stay here much longer you'll go slitty-eyed' (China, 1986), at which his hosts professed to take no offence at all since they habitually described westerners as 'round-eyed.'[§]

The shock and surprise that the Duke has brought the nation over the years accurately mirrors the role that he has played in his wife's life – never a dull moment. Lord Mountbatten liked to relate how, one weekend at Broadlands, he was crammed sideways in the back of an open top sports car being driven rapidly across the estate by Philip, with the Queen sitting in the front beside him. Every time they squealed round a corner, Elizabeth would show her alarm with an increasingly loud and 'aahing' intake of breath.

Suddenly Philip slammed on the brakes.

'If you make that bloody noise one more time,' he said, 'you'll have to get out and walk.'

The rest of the drive proceeded in silence, and when they reached their destination Philip got out of the car and stalked off.

'My dear,' protested Lord Mountbatten, as he struggled out of his cramped seat in the back. 'You're the Queen! Why do you let him treat you like that?'

'It's quite simple,' said Elizabeth, smiling happily, 'I didn't want to walk!'

---

§ Prince Philip did not spare his own family. He described the Windsor Great Park home of Prince Andrew and Fergie as resembling 'a tart's bedroom', and of his horse-mad daughter, Princess Anne, he once explained, 'If it doesn't fart or eat hay, she isn't interested.'

In sixty-four years of loving marriage Queen Elizabeth II has learned to tolerate much – not least her husband's delight in the company of pretty women. The Prince has heard all the rumours, and he laughs them off.

'He feels he's done nothing to feel guilty of,' says a close friend, 'so he doesn't give a damn what the world thinks.'

For many years Philip spent extra time with his cousin, Princess Alexandra, and for the last fifteen years or so his regular companion for weekends away has been another member of the family, his fellow carriage-driving enthusiast, Penelope, Lady Knatchbull, the attractive blonde wife of Lord Mountbatten's grandson (and Prince Philip's godson) Norton Knatchbull. Lady Knatchbull travelled around Britain with the Prince to compete in the four-in-hand driving events that replaced polo in the Prince's life, and the Queen was said to be content.

'She knows,' says one close female relative, 'there is no way he will humiliate her.'

When Norton Knatchbull deserted Broadlands and his wife in 2010 to go and live in the Bahamas with Jeannie McQueeny, the Nassau resort wear designer, Elizabeth made a point of inviting Penelope to join the Royal Family at Sandringham during the next New Year holidays. Sunday 9th January 2011 was a sunny day and most of the house party elected to walk to church. But the Queen chose to go by car with just one companion who was duly photographed by the waiting press – Penny Knatchbull.

For a quarter of her reign the world focused on the extraordinary marriage between her eldest son and Diana Spencer, but the reign's more extraordinary marriage has been between Prince Philip and the woman he calls 'Cabbage'. Elizabeth understands how a proud man who once captained his own ship might have difficulties perpetually staying one step behind her – a duty Prince Philip has performed for sixty-five years with graceful dedication – and she is too wise to feel

STRENGTH AND STAY.
Elizabeth II and Prince Philip enjoy the annual Trooping the Colour ceremony together on Horse Guards Parade. 13ᵗʰ June 2009

threatened by whatever he might need to do to prove his independence.

'He is someone who does not take easily to compliments,' declared the Queen at their Golden Wedding celebrations in 1997, 'but he has, quite simply, been my strength and stay all these years.'

It is at Balmoral on a warm autumn evening infested with gnats that Prince Philip comes into his own as the paterfamilias. Ever practical, ever tinkering, he is the proud deviser of a bulky, wheeled picnic trailer whose grilling rack and pots and pans are stowed neat and shipshape, with padded drawers for carefully segregated types of fortifying alcohol.

There are no servants in sight as the Duke dispenses his sausages, and afterwards it is the Queen who takes charge of the washing up – telling guests, politely but firmly, to stay away from the sink.

When the weather is colder, the party moves indoors, with after dinner parlour games. One involves miming words and phrases – 'food for thought', 'the top of the tree' – and when the game is over, visiting preachers are challenged by mischievous younger members of the family to see how many of the expressions they can fit into their sermon next morning.

'The record,' says one prince who likes to keep the score in church, 'is eleven.'

The legendary royal evening amusement is 'The Game', in which guests write the names of famous people on sticky labels and put them into a hat – Socrates, Napoleon, Gertrude Stein, Marilyn Monroe. You then draw out a label, stick it on your forehead and try to work out who you are by asking questions of your fellow players, to which they can only answer yes or no. Everyone did well on a recent evening, except for the unfortunate player who drew 'Geri Halliwell', and Prince Andrew took a closer look to see who had written the name on the label.

'That was you,' he said accusingly to his mother. 'I recognise the handwriting!'

'Well,' said the Queen defiantly, 'Geri Halliwell's a famous person, isn't she?'

There were live trees in the Abbey on 29th April 2011, and afterwards a churchwarden was caught executing a cartwheel of joy down the nave. The ridiculous secrecy surrounding the wedding dress made it seem that the garment must be a sacred icon, and everyone hoped that the randy best man would get off with the elegant maid of honour. The occasion nearly proved too much for the littlest bridesmaid, and there was a terrible row over the invitation list.

Apart from the live trees and the cartwheels, the cheering crowds and the 24 million TV viewers watching in Britain alone, the marriage of Prince William and Catherine Middleton was much like any other wedding in its joy and celebration of love and human commitment – and the triumph was very much that of Queen Elizabeth II. The Dean of Westminster invoked the idea of the 'mystical union' between Christ and the church but, as Jonathan Freedland

NEW GENERATION.
Prince William and Kate Middleton attend a friend's wedding shortly before the 16th November announcement of their own engagement. 23rd October 2010

remarked in the often monarchy-sceptical *Guardian*, the Dean could just as easily have been describing the 'mystical union' that exists between Britain and the Royal Family.

'What we witnessed was the mysterious alchemy that somehow converts love of country into affection for the House of Windsor.'

The last time Prince William had made a major appearance at the Abbey had been to bury his mother, and there were some at that time who had felt an inclination to bury the monarchy as well. Now here were Charles and, yes, a smiling Camilla in cream silk cheered on by the crowds as the pair of them 'gave away' Diana's eldest son in marriage. And the bride wore Diana's stunning sapphire engagement ring.

These were lessons of time and forgiveness and constancy to ponder, made flesh by the fallible and – what was the word? – 'dysfunctional' House of Windsor. No wonder Queen Elizabeth II had a smile on her face.

Ten days later she enjoyed another triumph when she travelled to Dublin with her husband on the first visit to Ireland by a British monarch for almost one hundred years. Her grandfather King George V, 'Grandpa England' to whom she used to wave across Green Park on winter mornings, travelled to Dublin in July 1911, where he received a greeting of 'almost unparalleled magnificence,' according to reports of the time, with crowds lining the seven-mile route from Kingstown (Dun Laoghaire) to the centre of Dublin.

In May 2011 the crowds were held back, for the most part, due to security concerns, since the intervening century had been marked by such events as the Easter Rising of 1916, the battle to establish the Irish Free State, and the war fought by the Irish Republican Army for the liberation of Northern Ireland from British rule. The 'Troubles' from the 1960s onwards had provided a catalogue of death and conflict, all of it occurring on her watch: the massacre of Bloody Sunday, the hunger strike of Bobby Sands, numerous IRA bombings and fatalities in England and, so painfully for the Royal Family, the murder of Lord Mountbatten and other members of his family in August 1979.

Northern Ireland had been the most deadly and intractable of the long-running sores of Elizabeth's reign, comparable to UDI and the fate of apartheid South Africa, but the more tragic for involving the make-up and loyalties of Great Britain itself. Every one of Elizabeth's later prime ministers had been frustrated by the Irish problem – Margaret Thatcher had nearly been killed by it – until April 1998 when Tony Blair and Bertie Ahern, the Irish Prime Minister, brought about the Good Friday Agreement. Elizabeth's visit, thirteen years later, was the fruit of the tough talking and paperwork that she had followed via 'the boxes' for so many decades. It meant a lot to Ireland, but it also meant a great deal to her.

'This was like a big door opening up for her,' said Prince William, 'that had been locked for so long.'

She dressed in green. The bookmakers had put huge odds on it. But there was still a gasp of pleasure when she emerged from her plane on Tuesday 17th May 2011 in a matching green hat and overcoat. When she rose to her feet to address the state banquet in Dublin Castle, her white formal dress was a mass of embroidered shamrocks, and she started with some words of Gaelic – her own idea and executed in an immaculate accent – 'A Uachtarán agus cairde,' 'President and friends.'

'Wow!' mouthed the President, Mary McAleese, in delighted astonishment. When Elizabeth finished speaking the whole room stood and applauded – 'not just polite applause,' wrote the *Irish Independent*, 'but sustained, heartfelt appreciation of the bridge that the Queen herself had built ... She had the look of a woman for whom the weight of history had just got a lot lighter.'

Some felt that her reference to 'things we wish had been done differently or not at all,' could have been fashioned into a more obvious apology. But when she went to the National Garden of Remembrance for those who died fighting the British, she bowed her head in deliberate and clearly sincere mourning. The pain and sadness etched into the Queen's features in repose can convey a powerful message.

EMBRACE OF NATIONS.

Elizabeth II speaks a little Irish at the State Banquet in Dublin Castle wearing a dress featuring 2,091 hand-embroidered shamrocks, with an Irish harp brooch of Swarovski crystals. Her 'Girls of Great Britain and Ireland' tiara was a wedding gift from her grandmother, Queen Mary. 18th May 2011

'That was the moment,' said Dinny McGinley, the Minister for Gaeltacht Affairs, 'when the whole nation lost a heartbeat.'

In Cork she plunged unprompted towards the waiting crowds with an enthusiasm worthy of Diana, chatting to the children from St Oliver's School.

'It's a day they will remember all their lives,' said their headmaster, Jim Daly. 'She's disarmed us completely. For all of us, on both sides of the divide, this visit has helped us reappraise our history and our culture – it's gone a long, long way to healing the wounds of past years.'

It all added up to a state visit unlike any other the Queen had undertaken – and it had also yielded a long-yearned-for personal treat. As long as the 'Troubles' lasted, Elizabeth II had not thought it proper to visit the legendary horse farms and bloodstock estates of southern Ireland: home to some of the finest racehorses in the world. Now she was due to visit three of them in a matter of days.

In the months before she travelled, Elizabeth had gone to great lengths to pick out the farms and the horses that she particularly wanted to inspect, and her personal pleasure only added to the triumph of the trip. After decades of bitterness and suspicion, the Queen's state visit to Ireland in May 2011 turned out to be, as her grandson William put it, a 'massive deal … cementing the fact that everyone should look for better things.' In the sixtieth year of her reign, on the eve of her Diamond Jubilee, Queen Elizabeth II had yet again demonstrated her command of the ultimate caring profession – to enable the embrace of nations.

Sources

This book is based on my previously published books *Majesty* (1977) and *Monarch* (2002 – published as *Royal* in the United Kingdom). Like those books, *A Brief Life of The Queen* includes numerous confidential interviews with advisors, friends and members of the Royal Family that were conducted on an off-the-record basis. The direct quotations in this book that are not identified in the notes below come from those unattributed interviews.

Chapter 1 – Princess of Hearts 1926–1947

paradise to inhabit	Woolf, Virginia, 'Royalty' in *The Moment and Other Essays* (London: Hogarth Press, 1947) p.230
sea-lions	Bradford, Sarah, *George VI* (London: Penguin, 2011) p.98
pink cherub	Ring, Anne, *The Story of Princess Elizabeth* (London: John Murray, 1932) p.54
fashion trend	*TIME* Magazine, 29 April 1929
sandpies	Pope-Hennessy, James, *Queen Mary: 1867–1953* (London: Allen & Unwin, 1959) p.546
all the equipment	Duchess of York to Cosmo Lang, 10 September 1930, Lambeth Palace Library, Lang Papers, in Shawcross, William, *Queen Elizabeth the Queen Mother: The Official Biography* (London: Pan, 2010) p.320
terrible	Wheeler-Bennett, John, *King George VI: His Life and Reign* (New York: St Martin's Press, 1958) p.258
placards	Orwell, George, *As I Please, 1943–1945: The Collected Essays, Journalism & Letters, Vol. 3* (San Diego: Harcourt, 1968) pp.17–18
upper classes	*Ibid.*
hatless	Betjeman, John, 'On the Death of George V', in Rose, Kenneth, *King George V* (London: Weidenfeld & Nicolson, 2000) Epilogue
not the person	*Birmingham Post,* 7 December 1936
intelligentsia	Attlee, Clement, *As It Happened* (London: Odhams Press, 1954) p.86

'The Choice'   *Punch,* 9 December 1936

Queen?   Pimlott, Ben, *The Queen: A Biography of Elizabeth II*
                      (London: HarperCollins, 2002) p.41

so much character   Sitwell, Osbert, *Rat Week: An Essay on the Abdication*
                      (London: Michael Joseph, 1986) p.44

misty morning   'From Lilibet, by Herself', Royal Archives, in
                      Pimlott, p.45

Finis   *Ibid.*

collective unconscious Jennings, Humphrey and Madge, Charles, *May the
                      Twelfth: Mass-Observation Day-Surveys by Over Two
                      Hundred Observers* (London: Faber & Faber, 1937)
                      p.45

true feelings   *Ibid.* p.304

centuries ago   *Ibid.* p.315

wondered why   *Ibid.* p.307

light reading   Shawcross, p.335

P.G. Wodehouse   'Owen Morshead to Queen Mary', 25 July 1941,
                      Royal Archives, in Shawcross, p.335

'serious' work   'Marion Crawford to Lady Cynthia Colville', 8
                      November 1937, Royal Archives, in Shawcross, p.334

Racing Demon   *Ibid.* p.334

fatal proceeding   'Queen Mary to Owen Morshead', 26 March 1941,
                      Royal Archives, in Shawcross, p.335

child-raising principles 'Notes by the Duchess of York', 1931–6, Royal
                      Archives, in Shawcross, p.336

growing up   Hulton Picture Archive, 96f/29/huch/462/11, April
                      1939

no question   Lascelles, Alan, 1938, Royal Archives, in Lacey,
                      Robert, *Monarch* (New York: Free Press, 2002) p.133

sloppy sentiment   Colville, John, *The Fringes of Power: Downing
                      Street Diaries 1939–1955* (London: Weidenfeld &
                      Nicolson, 2004) pp.165–166

some bulletins   Richards, Jeffrey and Sheridan, Dorothy, *Mass-
                      Observation at the Movies* (London & New York:
                      Routledge & Kegan Paul, 1987) p.162

symbol of the country *Ibid.* p.414

pocket money   Bradford, Sarah, *Elizabeth* (London: Penguin, 2002)
                      p.95

underworld   Crawford, Marion, *Little Princesses* (London: Cassell
                      & Co., 1951) p.70

one corgi   *Ibid.* pp.71–72

horses and dogs	Smith, Horace, *A Horseman Through Six Reigns: Reminiscences of a Royal Riding Master* (London: Odhams Press, 1955) p.45
special favourite	Shawcross, p.579
first meeting	Wheeler-Bennett, p.749
Viking	Crawford, p.59 ff.
starved of colour	'Queen Elizabeth to Queen Mary', 12 December 1943, Royal Archives, in Shawcross, p.578
Nippon	Shawcross, p.576
gramophone	'Princess Elizabeth to Marion Crawford', 1 January 1944, Royal Archives, in Shawcross, p.578
capered	Lascelles, Alan (ed. Duff Hart-Davis), *King's Counsellor: The Wartime Diaries of Sir Alan Lascelles* (London: Weidenfeld & Nicolson, 2006) p.189
woodpile	Pimlott, p.97
eighteen months	Longford, Elizabeth, *The Queen Mother: A Biography* (London: HarperCollins, 1981) p.106
rumour	Wheeler-Bennett, p.749
too young for that now	*Ibid.*
altogether wise?	Crawford, p.92
bushy beard	*Ibid.*
predictions	*New York Journal American,* 15 December 1943
ATS	Bradford, *Elizabeth* p.107
We want the King!	Wheeler-Bennett, p.626
official denial	Lacey, Robert, *Majesty* (London: Hutchinson, 1977) p.159
formally proposed	Shawcross, p.624
two celebrations	Airlie, Mabell, *Thatched With Gold* (London: Hutchinson, 1962) p.226
I declare	Morrah, Dermot, *The Royal Family in Africa* (London: Hutchinson, 1947) p.124
I wept	'Queen Mary to Queen Elizabeth', 22 April 1947, Royal Archives, in Shawcross, p.107
old bores	'Sir Alan Lascelles to Lady Lascelles', 30 April 1947, Churchill College Archives, Cambridge, in Shawcross, p.107
admirable technique	*Ibid.*

Chapter 2 – A delighted sort of family feeling 1947–1953

twelve weeks away	Shawcross, p.636
wrote to apologise	*Ibid.* p.625
the right decision	*Ibid.* p.626

feelings for her daughter	*Ibid.* p.625
new life together	*Ibid.* p.626
made up her mind	*Ibid.*
'Where's Philip?'	Crawford, p.100
fond of him	Shawcross, p.626
the betrothal	Lacey, *Majesty* p.164
make an impression	Airlie, p.228
makeshift weddings	Ziegler, Philip, *Crown and People* (New York: Knopf, 1987) p.81
'Let her alone'	News Quota, Mass-Observation Archive, Sussex University, 12 October 1947
Lyons silk	Pimlott, p.127
Nationalist silkworms	Hartnell, Norman, *Silver and Gold* (London: Pitman Publishing, 1956) p.113
the monarchy's work	*Ibid.*
nylon stockings	Lacey, *Majesty* p.169
family feeling	Diaries, Mass-Observation Archive, Sussex University, November 1947
something very precious	Wheeler-Bennett, pp.754–5
'Royal Family'	*Ibid.*
love and fairness	'Princess Elizabeth to Queen Elizabeth', 22 November 1947, Royal Archives, in Shawcross, p.630
darling little daughter	'Queen Elizabeth to Princess Elizabeth', 24 November 1947, Royal Archives, in Shawcross, p.630
doting grandmother	'Queen Elizabeth to Princess Elizabeth', 7 April 1951, Royal Archives, in Shawcross, p.645
Accession Declaration	Author's interview with Lord Charteris
talked to her	Author's interview with Michael Parker
accepting her destiny	Author's interview with Lord Charteris
she had been crying	Dean, John, *HRH Prince Philip, Duke of Edinburgh* (London: Robert Hale Press, 1954) p.148
a personal loss	Ziegler, *Crown and People* p.85
still got Churchill	*Ibid.*
'God Save the Queen!'	Macmillan, Harold, *Tides of Fortune* (London: Macmillan, 1969) p.372
the new renaissance	Lacey, *Majesty* p.194
tickets were selling	*Ibid.* p.192
impossibly 'common'	Author's interview with Michael Parker
the great dangers	Barker, Brian, *When the Queen Was Crowned* (London: Routledge, 1976) p.53
a foolish deed undone	*Daily Express,* 21 October 1952
solemn promises	Lacey, *Majesty* p.198

Chapter 3 – New Elizabethans 1953–1969

circus of a civilization	Maschler, Tom (ed.), *Declaration* (London: MacGibbon & Kee, 1957) pp.76–77
a watching journalist	Lacey, *Majesty* p.211
multi-racial make-up	*National and English Review,* May 1953
a priggish schoolgirl	*Ibid.* August 1957
either mad or bad	Peter Townsend, *Time and Chance: An Autobiography* (London: Collins, 1978) p.198
sympathetic acceptance	*Ibid.* p.197
Margaret surrendered	Shawcross, p.700
Christian marriage	Lacey, *Majesty* p.252
life in a cottage	Author's interview with Kenneth Rose
lied to the Queen	Author's interview with Lord Mountbatten, 1976
Sèvres	Shlaim, Avi, 'The Protocol of Sèvres, 1956: Anatomy of a War Plot,' *International Affairs,* Vol. 73, No. 3 (1997) pp.509–530
a surprising consensus	Maxwell Fyfe, David, *Political Adventure* (London: Weidenfeld & Nicolson, 1964) p.285
'The Establishment'	'Political Commentary', *The Spectator,* 23 September 1955
'Annus Mirabilis'	Larkin, Philip, 'Annus Mirabilis', *High Windows* (London: Faber & Faber, 1974) p.34
prime ministerial lip	Wilson, Harold, *The Labour Government 1964–1970* (London: Weidenfeld & Nicolson, 1971) p.1
the Bletchley area	Author's interview with Lord Wilson
do his homework	Wilson, Harold, Speech in Downing Street, 23 March 1976
sharpening a knife	Lacey, *Majesty* p.320
down on the floor	Benn, Tony, *Out of the Wilderness: Diaries 1963–1967* (London: Arrow, 1988) p.232
off the stamps	*Ibid.* p.361
South Wales	Author's interview with Lord Charteris
no vanity	*Ibid.*
anti-Press Secretary	*Ibid.*
rather an advantage	Author's interview with Sir William Heseltine
'Will we have some say?'	Author's interview with Lord Brabourne
'a candle snuffer'	Coward, Noël, (eds. Payne, Graham and Morley, Sheridan), *The Noël Coward Diaries* (London: Weidenfeld & Nicolson, 1982) p.678
revival of interest	*Yorkshire Post,* 23 June 1969
'royalty mania'	*Sunday Times,* 29 June 1969

Chapter 4 – Daylight in upon magic 1969–1981

Happy crowds	Dimbleby, Jonathan, *The Prince of Wales: A Biography* (London: Little, Brown, 1994) p.165
a self-pitying character	*Spectator* interview, 1995, quoted in 'Queen's confidant dies', BBC News, 24 December 1999
his mother's parenting	Dimbleby, p.59
Fleet coverage	*Ibid.* p.165
'affection and appreciation'	*Ibid.* p.189
sweet-charactered girl	Author's interview with Lord Mountbatten
'Edward the Caresser'	Lees-Milne, James, *The Enigmatic Edwardian* (London: Sidgwick & Jackson, 1986) p.206
healthy sex life	Author's interview with Lord Mountbatten
lost his heart	Dimbleby, p.221
daylight upon magic	Bagehot, Walter, *The English Constitution* (Oxford: Oxford University Press, 2001) p.54
Commonwealth Conference	Author's interview with Lord Charteris
insensitive pay claim	'Select Committee on the Civil List', Hansard Archives, 1971, p.xlvii
kept woman	'Civil List Debate', Hansard Archives, 14 December 1971, columns 278–400
Inland Revenue	Hall, Phillip, *Royal Fortune* (London: Bloomsbury, 1992) p.65
'I don't agree'	Pimlott, p.406
'venomous observations'	Shawcross, p.843
laying down wine	'Select Committee on the Civil List', 1971, p.9
'lowest of the low'	'Notes by Queen Elizabeth II', 6 July 1940, Royal Archives in Shawcross, p.520
grandmother's enmity	Dimbleby, p.215
tears in her eyes	Bloch, Michael, *The Secret File on the Duke of Windsor* (London: Bantam Press, 1988) p.302
nanny-like tenderness	Bradford, *Elizabeth* p.415
'a carpet of happiness'	Author's interview with Lord Charteris
half-hearted affairs	De Courcy, Anne, *Snowdon: The Biography* (London: Weidenfeld & Nicolson, 2008) p.145
'If it moves'	*Ibid.* p.37
a Jewish manicurist	*Ibid.* p.177
'Titles?'	*Daily Mail,* 23 January 1981
some glee	Author's interview with Joe Haines
Porchie	Hoey, Brian, *Her Majesty* (London: HarperCollins, 2001) p.247
I can feel it	Mass-Observation Archive, Diary Files, Silver Jubilee

symphony concert	*Private Eye,* 18 February 1977
working class culture	*Ibid.*
'CRISIS? WHAT CRISIS?'	Rees, Nigel, The *"Quote ... Unquote" Newsletter,* Vol. 20, No. 4 (October, 2011) p.1
the Iron Lady	Author's interview with Lord Bell
Nanny being there	Author's interview with Lord Charteris
Greedy Mendicants	*The Windsors: A Royal Family,* PBS Video, 1994
Coons Holidaying	Thatcher, Carol, *Below the Parapet – The Biography of Denis Thatcher* (London: HarperCollins, 1997) p.152
her duty to go	Author's interview with Lord Carington
elections coming up	Bradford, *Elizabeth* p.384
desperate emotions	Dimbleby, p.324
disgraceful abdication	Ziegler, Philip, *Mountbatten* (New York: Knopf, 1985) p.686

Chapter 5 – Whatever 'in love' means 1981–1995

Chitty Chitty Bang Bang	Morton, Andrew, *Diana: Her True Story – In Her Own Words* (London: Michael O'Mara, 2003) p.26
English schoolgirl	Dimbleby, pp.338-339
police contacts	Author's interview with James Whitaker
that spectacular	Clayton, Tim and Craig, Phil, *Diana: Story of a Princess* (London: Hodder & Stoughton, 2001) p.42
fabulous bazookahs	Brandreth, Gyles, *Charles and Camilla* (London: Arrow, 2005) p.220
cool as a cucumber	*News of the World,* 14 June 1981
difficult Prince	Morton, p.33
doing privately	*Ibid.*
going to hunt	*Ibid.* p.38
filthy row	*Ibid.* p.37
total jealousy	*Ibid.* p.39
'Girl Friday'	Dimbleby, p.347
I dreamt of Camilla	Morton, p.43
sort me out	*Ibid.* p.44
pompous remark	Author's interviews with two of the editors at the meeting
ears like his father	Morton, p.138
Elizabeth Regina	*Daily Express,* 24 September 1982
hell would break loose	Keay, Douglas, *Elizabeth II: Portrait of a Monarch* (London: Century, 1991) p.238
a smacking naval kiss	*The Times,* 24 July 1986
a religious person?	Pimlott, p.496

I have sailed *Britannia*	*Ibid.* p.515
positive titbits	Author's interviews with Michael Shea
she went out of her way	Pimlott, p.513
last bloody thing	*Ibid.* p.510
back to the camera	Brown, Tina, *The Diana Chronicles* (London: Arrow, 2011) p.251
mission to save	Author's interview with Richard Kay
chose to send Diana	Bradford, Sarah, *Diana* (London: Penguin, 2007) p.169
spicy shampoo	Berry, Wendy, *The Housekeeper's Diary: Charles and Diana Before the Breakup* (New York: Barricade Books, 1995) p.56
words in the paper	*Diana: Story of a Princess* (Part 2), ITV, 2005
live inside your trousers	Whitaker, James, *Diana vs. Charles: Royal Blood Feud* (New York: Dutton, 1993) p.19
Annus horrendus	Rees, Nigel, *Brewer's Dictionary of Famous Quotations* (London: Weidenfeld & Nicolson, 2006) p.187
have a drink	Shawcross, p.894
time in prison	Sampson, Anthony, *Mandela: The Authorised Biography* (London: HarperCollins, 2000) p.xxv
colour-blind	Author's interview with Lord Owen

Chapter 6 – As your Queen and as a grandmother 1995–2012

the right thing	Dimbleby, p.342
deep friendship	*Ibid.* p.335
very let down	BBC, *Panorama*, 'Transcript of Martin Bashir's interview with the Princess of Wales' (1995)
Love from Mama	Burrell, Paul, *A Royal Duty* (London: Penguin, 2004) p.222
radios out of their rooms	These descriptions of Balmoral and Buckingham Palace in the days following Diana's death are based on off-the-record interviews with people who were there and closely involved in events
People's Princess	*The Sun,* 4th September 1997
this thing of the flag	Author's interview with Alastair Campbell
as a grandmother	www.sweetspeeches.com, 'The Queen's Speech Following the Death of Princess Diana' (1997)
This was London	Author's interview with Peter Edwards
She's back in charge	Author's interview with Arthur Edwards
the occasional corgi	Hardman, Robert, *Our Queen* (London: Hutchinson, 2011) p.154

Tony Blair	Author's interview with Alastair Campbell
David Cameron	Hardman, p.153
friendliness	Sarah Bradford, 'Meeting the Monarch,' *The Telegraph,* 28th June 2007
the casket	Shawcross, pp.929–937
young bloke	Hardman, p.55
never lived together	*Daily Mirror,* 7 January 1999
work it out	Hardman, p.35
manifold sins	BBC History, 'Prince Charles and Camilla Parker Bowles' Wedding' (2005)
Pebbles?	*Daily Mail,* 10 June 2011, 'As Prince Philip Turns 90, Relive Some of his Most Hilarious Gaffes' (2011)
didn't want to walk	Author's interview with Lord Mountbatten
mysterious alchemy	Freedland, Jonathan, 'The Wedding Speaks Volumes,' *Guardian,* 30 April 2011
door opening	Hardman, p.53
healing the wounds	Bates, Stephen, 'Queen Shaken and Stirred,' *Guardian,* 20 May 2011

Further Reading

I warmly commend any and all of the books cited in these notes (for full publication details, look for the very first reference to the author). Modesty does not prevent me from mentioning my own most recent full length work, *Monarch* (New York: Free Press, 2002), published in Great Britain as *Royal* (London: Little Brown, 2002), on some of which this brief life is based. If I were asked to recommend just one book about the Queen, it would have to be the updated Golden Jubilee edition of the thoughtful and masterful biography by the late Ben Pimlott (London: HarperCollins, 2002). On the events of the Charles and Diana years, see *The Diana Chronicles,* the consummate account by Tina Brown (London: Arrow, 2011). And the finest royal biography of all has to be Kenneth Rose's superb study of the Queen's grandfather *King George V* (London: Weidenfeld & Nicolson, 2000).

'Lege feliciter,' as the Venerable Bede would say – 'May you read happily.'